Ephesian Benchmarks: Sit-Walk-Stand

Christian Growth to Maturity

By Brother B

authorHOUSE®

AuthorHouse™
1663 Liberty Drive
Bloomington, IN 47403
www.authorhouse.com
Phone: 1-800-839-8640

First published by AuthorHouse 6/24/2010

ISBN: 978-1-4520-3541-3 (sc)
ISBN: 978-1-4520-3542-0 (e)

Library of Congress Control Number: 2010908069

Printed in the United States of America
Bloomington, Indiana

This book is printed on acid-free paper.

All scriptures quoted from the King James Version of the bible, unless noted otherwise.

Ephesian Benchmarks: Sit-Walk-Stand

Christian Growth to Maturity

Have you ever wondered how you can stand in the power of God's might? Many think believing in Jesus Christ and being born again provides us with all we need to be mighty warriors for God. However, that is not the case. After our new birth in Christ, we are described as newborn babes, not as warriors for God. There is a process of growth each believer must go through. There are no shortcuts to spiritual maturity.

The three key elements to guide us to maturity are outlined in a book by Watchman Nee, <u>Sit, Walk, Stand</u>, Tyndale House Publishers, 1977. Brother Nee was a Chinese disciple of the early half of the 20th century. He explained that the Christian life can be looked at in three distinct and progressive phases—sit, walk, and stand. A believer must first sit, a position of rest and observation, and understand all that Christ <u>has already done</u> for us. Note the tense is past, what He has already done for us, not what He will do for us. Having sat and gained an understanding of our position in Christ, we are then commanded to begin walking worthy of the One who has called us. Finally, we need to stand in the power of His might against all the wiles of the devil, and having done all—to stand.

These series of studies are organized around the three key benchmarks of sit, walk, and stand. They are designed for small group discussions or one-on-one studies between a mentor and a mentee. These studies were derived from a series of lessons given to men and women in prison to prepare them to continue their walk in Christ upon their release from prison.

I pray these studies will bless your heart as you learn to sit, walk, and stand in the power of His might. May all of the glory be to our Lord and Savior Jesus Christ.

In His service,
Brother Brothers

Ephesian Benchmarks: Sit-Walk-Stand

Study Outlines

Study 1: You Must Be Born Again

Ephesians 2:1-9

Ephesians 2:1-9 (chapter two, verses 1 through 9).

"1 And you hath he quickened, who were dead in trespasses and sins;

2 Wherein in time past ye walked according to the course of this world, according to the prince of the power of the air, the spirit that now worketh in the children of disobedience:

3 Among whom also we all had our conversation in times past in the lusts of our flesh, fulfilling the desires of the flesh and of the mind; and were by nature the children of wrath, even as others.

4 But God, who is rich in mercy, for his great love wherewith he loved us,

5 Even when we were dead in sins, hath quickened us together with Christ, (by grace ye are saved;)

6 And hath raised us up together, and made us sit together in heavenly places in Christ Jesus:

7 That in the ages to come he might shew the exceeding riches of his grace in his kindness toward us through Christ Jesus.

8 For by grace are ye saved through faith; and that not of yourselves: it is the gift of God:

9 Not of works, lest any man should boast." (KJV)

This first study begins in chapter two of Ephesians, because Paul deals with our spiritual condition before we were alive or born again in Christ. Once we understand our condition, then we can choose to make a change—going from death unto life. Once that issue is settled, then the study will examine some of the marvelous truths in chapter one.

This study is designed for your first face-to-face bible study time together. To help you get to know each other, I suggest you use the acronym "F.I.R.E.", which I have adapted from an old Southern Baptist "Continuing Witnessing Training" program. It should help lead our initial discussion, which is a general sharing time.

1. "F" stands for family, but here, let it also stand for future. Tell us about your background, your family, children, and the like. Tell us about your plans for the future such as your job and house plans.

_____

_____

_____

2. "I" stands for interests or hobbies. Tell about your interests and hobbies.

_____

_____

_____

3. "R" stands for religious background. When you attended church, where did you go? Tell me about any faith-based programs in which you participated.

_____

_____

_____

4. "E" stands for exploratory questions. There are two very important questions we would like you to answer.

    a. **<u>Question One</u>**: "Do you know for certain that if you died tonight that you would go to heaven?" What would your answer be?

_____

_____

_____

    b. **<u>Question Two</u>**: "Suppose you are standing before God right now, and He asks you, 'Why should I let you into My heaven?'" What would you tell Him?

_____

_____

_____

5. In Ephesians 2:1 and 5, it talks about us being dead in trespasses and sins. In your opinion, what do you think that means?

_____

_____

_____

6. List the things that a dead person can do.

_____

_____

_____

7. If we are dead in trespasses and sins, how do we become alive or quickened by God?

_____

_____

_____

8. Ephesians 2:8 says, "For by grace are ye saved through faith; and that not of yourselves: it is the gift of God." Based on this verse, how is one saved?

_____

_____

_____

9. Looking at Ephesians 2:8 again, "For by grace are ye saved through faith; and that not of yourselves: it is the gift of God," what do you think the word "it" refers to?

_____

_____

_____

10. What is your understanding of Ephesians 2:9, "Not of works, lest any man should boast."

_____

_____

_____

11. Ephesians 2:6 is the first occurrence of the word "sit". What do you think the phrase, "made us **sit together** in the heavenly places in Christ Jesus" means?

_____

_____

_____

You must remember where Christ is seated—at the throne of God the Father. We are given the amazing privilege to be seated with Him. We are in a place of extreme high honor. Our next study will examine more about what "sit together" means.

Study 2: Sit and Learn What God Has Already Done
Ephesians 1:1-12

Ephesians 1:1-12

"1   Paul, an apostle of Jesus Christ by the will of God, to the saints which are at Ephesus, and to the faithful in Christ Jesus:

2   Grace be to you, and peace, from God our Father, and from the Lord Jesus Christ.

3   Blessed be the God and Father of our Lord Jesus Christ, who hath blessed us with all spiritual blessings in heavenly places in Christ:

4   According as he hath chosen us in him before the foundation of the world, that we should be holy and without blame before him in love:

5   Having predestinated us unto the adoption of children by Jesus Christ to himself, according to the good pleasure of his will,

6   To the praise of the glory of his grace, wherein he hath made us accepted in the beloved.

7   In whom we have redemption through his blood, the forgiveness of sins, according to the riches of his grace;

8   Wherein he hath abounded toward us in all wisdom and prudence;

9   Having made known unto us the mystery of his will, according to his good pleasure which he hath purposed in himself:

10 That in the dispensation of the fulness of times he might gather together in one all things in Christ, both which are in heaven, and which are on earth; even in him:

11 In whom also we have obtained an inheritance, being predestinated according to the purpose of him who worketh all things after the counsel of his own will:

12 That we should be to the praise of his glory, who first trusted in Christ." (KJV)

This study is the beginning of one of the great doctrinal passages in the New Testament. It begins to explain why God has "made us sit together in the heavenly places in Christ Jesus." If you were invited to the White House to sit next to the President, what would your reaction be? I know I would be in awe, yet very excited, and nervous. Would you have a lot to share with the President? I think I would keep my mouth shut and listen to what all the other high officials and the President were saying. This too is the primary reason we are made to sit together—we are to observe, listen and keep quiet.

God wants us to know what has already been done on our behalf. Ephesians 1:3 begins this key revelation. Note it is past tense. He has already given all of the spiritual blessings to those of us who are IN CHRIST JESUS. Ephesians 1:4 through 12 give us a list of what these blessings are.

1. According to Ephesians 1:4 and 5, when did God choose you? And what was His purpose in choosing you?

_____

_____

_____

2. If someone becomes adopted, what does that mean?

_____

_____

_____

3. In the last part of Ephesians 1:6, occurs an interesting concept: ". . . wherein he hath made us accepted in the beloved." What do you think it means?

_____

_____

_____

4. In Ephesians 1:7-12, list the blessings identified there.

_____

_____

_____

5. In Ephesians 1:5 and 11, the concept of predestined is introduced. What do you think it means?

_____

_____

_____

6. Predestined means pre-determined or decided before the event ever occurs. What caused God to pre-determine or pre-decide to pick you as one of His adopted children?

_____

_____

_____

7. When you look over this passage, what is the most important "blessing" to you personally?

_____

_____

_____

Finally, remember God has blessed us (past tense) with "all spiritual blessings in heavenly places in Christ Jesus". The word "all" means God has provided every blessing available to us today. Take the opportunity right now to give thanks and praise to God for what He has already done for us!

Study 3: Continue to Sit and Be Enlightened

Ephesians 1:13-23

Ephesians 1:13-23

"13 In whom ye also trusted, after that ye heard the word of truth, the gospel of your salvation: in whom also after that ye believed, ye were sealed with that Holy Spirit of promise,

14 Which is the earnest of our inheritance until the redemption of the purchased possession, unto the praise of his glory.

15 Wherefore I also, after I heard of your faith in the Lord Jesus, and love unto all the saints,

16 Cease not to give thanks for you, making mention of you in my prayers;

17 That the God of our Lord Jesus Christ, the Father of glory, may give unto you the spirit of wisdom and revelation in the knowledge of him:

18 The eyes of your understanding being enlightened; that ye may know what is the hope of his calling, and what the riches of the glory of his inheritance in the saints,

19 And what is the exceeding greatness of his power to us-ward who believe, according to the working of his mighty power,

20 Which he wrought in Christ, when he raised him from the dead, and set him at his own right hand in the heavenly places,

21 Far above all principality, and power, and might, and dominion, and every name that is named, not only in this world, but also in that which is to come:

22 And hath put all things under his feet, and gave him to be the head over all things to the church,

23 Which is his body, the fulness of him that filleth all in all." (KJV)

1. This study starts with one of the crucial passages to help us understand the process of salvation. Ephesians 1:13 and 14 are the key. Paul gives us a definite order of events to the new birth here. Please list them.

_____

_____

_____

2. But as we said in the previous study, we were dead in sins and trespasses, so how is it that we are able to hear the Word of God?

_____

_____

_____

When we make the choice to believe and put the full weight of our faith in Christ, then God does something else—He seals us with the Holy Spirit of promise. We have forgotten what seals are all about. In ancient times, a seal was made that uniquely represented the power and authority of the ruler. In Christ's burial, they sealed the tomb with the royal seal of Rome. If anyone tampered with the grave or broke the seal, they would be subject to the full weight of Roman law against the perpetrator. God has decided to place a mark or seal on each of us who hear and believe the Gospel. It is a down payment, an earnest payment, whereby God says "You are mine and know that I have redeemed you forever."

3. If God has placed His seal on you, what else has occurred?

_____

_____

_____

4. This manifestation of the Holy Spirit is different to each believer. In my case, the first indication was the lifting of the crushing burden of guilt I felt. Look at 2 Corinthians 5:17 and write what it says in your own words.

_____

_____

_____

Another benefit I recognized was the complete peace that was suddenly in my heart. I had been in a horrible hurricane that threatened to break my very small boat in pieces. It was a dark, raging storm. Yet, shortly after receiving Christ, I felt in my heart that there was total tranquility. The waters were perfectly calm, and the wind had stopped. The top of the water became like a mirror. I could see reflections all the way across to the other side. For the first time in my life, in my heart of hearts that only I knew about, there was a wonderful, indescribable peace. Much later, I came across this marvelous promise:

John 14:27
"27 Peace I leave with you, my peace I give unto you: not as the world giveth, give I unto you. Let not your heart be troubled, neither let it be afraid." (KJV)

5. What other indications have you discovered when you put your faith in Christ?

_____

_____

_____

6. Beginning in Ephesians 1:17 through 19, Paul lets us in on how he is praying for new believers. In verse 17, Paul lists three things he wanted God to give each believer. List them.

_____

_____

_____

7. In Ephesians 1:18 and 19, Paul asks that God would give each believer several additional items. List them.

_____

_____

_____

8. Of the ones you listed above, which one is the most important to you and why?

_____

_____

_____

Sit is the first process of Sit-Walk-Stand. Remember that God at different times in your journey will call you back to sit again and again. Relish these times of intimate fellowship and observation. Listen carefully and you will discover there are some things you were not ready to receive until this new time of sitting.

9. Summarize the things required to "sit" and list the key things you have learned.

_____

_____

_____

_____

_____

_____

_____

_____

_____

_____

_____

_____

_____

_____

_____

_____

_____

_____

Study 4: Preparing to Walk, but First—Remember

Ephesians 2:8-18

Ephesians 2:8-18

"8 For by grace are ye saved through faith; and that not of yourselves: it is the gift of God:

9   Not of works, lest any man should boast.

10 For we are his workmanship, created in Christ Jesus unto good works, which God hath before ordained that we should walk in them.

11 Wherefore remember, that ye being in time past Gentiles in the flesh, who are called Uncircumcision by that which is called the Circumcision in the flesh made by hands;

12 That at that time ye were without Christ, being aliens from the commonwealth of Israel, and strangers from the covenants of promise, having no hope, and without God in the world:

13 But now in Christ Jesus ye who sometimes were far off are made nigh by the blood of Christ.

14 For he is our peace, who hath made both one, and hath broken down the middle wall of partition between us;

15 Having abolished in his flesh the enmity, even the law of commandments contained in ordinances; for to make in himself of twain one new man, so making peace;

16 And that he might reconcile both unto God in one body by the cross, having slain the enmity thereby:

17 And came and preached peace to you which were afar off, and to them that were nigh.

18 For through him we both have access by one Spirit unto the Father." (KJV)

1. The first two verses of this study are very familiar to most evangelical Christians—Ephesians 2:8 and 9. But most who quote it forget to include verse 10. This presents the full picture of salvation and where faith and works fit in. Verses 8 and 9 say salvation is not earned by works, but rather by the exercise of faith. Yet having been saved, we are described as God's workmanship, prepared for doing good works. What do you think this means?

_____

_____

_____

In other words, faith alone brings salvation. But wait a minute. The epistle of James says just the opposite—faith without works is dead.

James 2:14-18

"14 What doth it profit, my brethren, though a man say he hath faith, and have not works? can faith save him?

15 If a brother or sister be naked, and destitute of daily food,

16 And one of you say unto them, Depart in peace, be ye warmed and filled; notwithstanding ye give them not those things which are needful to the body; what doth it profit?

17 Even so faith, if it hath not works, is dead, being alone.

18 Yea, a man may say, Thou hast faith, and I have works: shew me thy faith without thy works, and I will shew thee my faith by my works." (KJV)

2. How do you reconcile these two passages and concepts?

_____

_____

_____

But Ephesians 2:10 tells us what God expects of His children. We are His workmanship, created in Christ Jesus for the purpose of doing good works. Salvation is not earned by works, but once saved, God commands us to do good works. We are compelled to do good works, otherwise our faith is faulty and we are deceiving ourselves.

James 1:22
"22 But be ye doers of the word, and not hearers only, deceiving your own selves." (KJV)

3. How do you understand the term God's workmanship as applied to you?

_____

_____

_____

4. But before beginning the walk phase, Paul says to remember the way you were before you met Christ. Describe what you find in Ephesians 2:11-13.

_____

_____

_____

Before we knew Christ, we were outside God's promises of grace, mercy, and redemption—a hopeless situation. We were pursuing the wrong things in the world. James describes it this way.

James 4:4
"4 Ye adulterers and adulteresses, know ye not that the friendship of the world is enmity with God? whosoever therefore will be a friend of the world is the enemy of God." (KJV)

5. The love of the world makes us God's enemy. Look at 1 John 2:15-17 and describe what you find.

_____

_____

_____

Rather than spend your time in the world's philosophy, pursuing things that perish, focus on things above that can never be stolen, rusted out, or eaten by moths. This focus is possible as I enter into a relationship with Christ by accepting His blood sacrifice as payment for my sins as described in Ephesians 2:13.

6. The Old Testament pictures this through the Passover miracle that occurred when Moses was trying to convince the Pharaoh of Egypt to release the Israelite slaves from captivity. Look at Exodus 12:12-23 and describe what the blood on the door post of a house did.

_____

_____

_____

7. Now look at Colossians 2:13-14 and describe what else Christ has done in making you alive or quickened.

_____

_____

_____

You see, all your trespasses are forgiven and are nailed to His cross. As one hymn writer put it, "My sin, not in part, but the whole, is nailed to the cross and I bear it no more. Praise the Lord, praise the Lord, O my soul." (It Is Well With My Soul, Horatio Spafford.) We are no longer aliens and enemies of God, but rather he has adopted us as His sons, holy and without blame, walking before Him in love.

Another marvelous thing that this passage in Ephesians tells us is that the animosity between Jews and non-Jews has been eliminated. Even today, there is a great barrier between Jews and non-Jews. The war and terror in the world today have their roots in the conflict between the Jews and Arabs, both of which claim to be the chosen people of God. But Christ broke down that barrier by His blood, enabling all of mankind to be reconciled to God as one body or church. Each of us can have peace with God and each other, having access by the One Spirit to God the Father.

Study 5: God's Instrument for Your Walk—The Church

Ephesians 2:19-3:12

Ephesians 2:19-3:12

"19 Now therefore ye are no more strangers and foreigners, but fellowcitizens with the saints, and of the household of God;

20 And are built upon the foundation of the apostles and prophets, Jesus Christ himself being the chief corner stone;

21 In whom all the building fitly framed together groweth unto an holy temple in the Lord:

22 In whom ye also are builded together for an habitation of God through the Spirit.

CHAPTER 3

1 For this cause I Paul, the prisoner of Jesus Christ for you Gentiles,

2 If ye have heard of the dispensation of the grace of God which is given me to you-ward:

3 How that by revelation he made known unto me the mystery; (as I wrote afore in few words,

4 Whereby, when ye read, ye may understand my knowledge in the mystery of Christ)

5 Which in other ages was not made known unto the sons of men, as it is now revealed unto his holy apostles and prophets by the Spirit;

6 That the Gentiles should be fellowheirs, and of the same body, and partakers of his promise in Christ by the gospel:

7 Whereof I was made a minister, according to the gift of the grace of God given unto me by the effectual working of his power.

8 Unto me, who am less than the least of all saints, is this grace given, that I should preach among the Gentiles the unsearchable riches of Christ;

9 And to make all men see what is the fellowship of the mystery, which from the beginning of the world hath been hid in God, who created all things by Jesus Christ:

10 To the intent that now unto the principalities and powers in heavenly places might be known by the church the manifold wisdom of God,

11 According to the eternal purpose which he purposed in Christ Jesus our Lord:

12 In whom we have boldness and access with confidence by the faith of him." (KJV)

1. This study begins with "Now therefore", which means Paul is about to reveal information based on what he has just said previously. We, the Gentiles, are no longer a stranger or a foreigner, but fellow citizens with the saints and part of God's household. But in being part of God's household, God is in the process of building something. What is it?

_____

_____

_____

God begins to reveal one of His purposes for us—to become one of the building blocks used to build the great temple where God Himself will dwell forever. That temple is the church, the called out assembly of all believers of every tongue and nation under heaven. To form this temple, we must submit to Christ, the Master Architect, who is fitly joining and placing each of us into the temple in order for it to grow to completion.

2. This process is described in detail in 1 Corinthians 12:13-27. The One Spirit baptizes us into the body, assigning us our position and responsibilities. We are described as many members, yet one body. How are the different members supposed to support each other? Is one member more important than another?

_____

_____

_____

God has placed each of us in the body as it pleased Him. He made sure that everyone has a purpose to fulfill in the body. No one can say I do not need you. Without you functioning properly, then the body cannot function as God designed it.

3. Paul resumes the revelation of the purpose for the churches in Ephesians 3:3. There he describes the revelation of a "mystery", something hidden until now. What was revealed?

_____

_____

_____

4. Later in Ephesians 3:9, Paul describes something called "the fellowship of the mystery." What is he talking about?

_____

_____

_____

5. In Ephesians 3:10, Paul also talks about the "manifold wisdom of God". Look at the passage in 1 Corinthians 1:26-31 and describe what you find.

_____

_____

_____

The wise and the mighty things of this world are brought to nothing. God has made it available to all, not just the elite few. Note too in 1 Corinthians 1:30 the phrase "but of Him are you in Christ Jesus." Even our status in Christ is <u>not</u> of our own doing. There is simply no boasting at all about our position in Christ. It is <u>not</u> of our effort, but of God's divine work. Jesus is our wisdom, righteousness, sanctification, and redemption. All of our praise belongs to Him. I like the way Jeremiah describes it.

Jeremiah 9:23-24

"23 Thus saith the LORD, Let not the wise man glory in his wisdom, neither let the mighty man glory in his might, let not the rich man glory in his riches:

24 But let him that glorieth glory in this, that he understandeth and knoweth me, that I am the LORD which exercise lovingkindness, judgment, and righteousness, in the earth: for in these things I delight, saith the LORD. (KJV)

Note in verse 24 above the things that God takes a delight in: understanding and knowing God, who exercises lovingkindness, judgment, and righteousness. These are the attitudes and actions or works that God has ordained for us.

6. Another characteristic of the manifold wisdom of God through the church is love, rather than hate. This type of love is totally different than the world's view as explained by Christ in His sermon on the mount and in John's gospel. Look at Matthew 5:43-48 and describe what you find.

_____

_____

_____

Note that there is considerable difference between the world's idea of love expressed in Matthew and what God wants us to do. Loving your enemies and praying for them is very difficult for us, but is the standard God requires for those who are of His kingdom.

7. Finally, in Ephesians 3:12, Paul tells us some key things available to us who are in Christ Jesus. What are they?

_____

_____

_____

It is a marvelous privilege to be chosen to be part of God's revealed mystery. In case you missed it, our living testimony will give principalities and powers in the heavenly places reason to stop in awe and amazement and exclaim, "Oh, the manifold wisdom of God is so much more than we ever imagined, especially as revealed through these men and women who make up the church."

Study 6: Paul's Prayer for the Power to Walk

Ephesians 3:13-21

Ephesians 3:13-21

"13 Wherefore I desire that ye faint not at my tribulations for you, which is your glory.

14 For this cause I bow my knees unto the Father of our Lord Jesus Christ,

15 Of whom the whole family in heaven and earth is named,

16 That he would grant you, according to the riches of his glory, to be strengthened with might by his Spirit in the inner man;

17 That Christ may dwell in your hearts by faith; that ye, being rooted and grounded in love,

18 May be able to comprehend with all saints what is the breadth, and length, and depth, and height;

19 And to know the love of Christ, which passeth knowledge, that ye might be filled with all the fulness of God.

20 Now unto him that is able to do exceeding abundantly above all that we ask or think, according to the power that worketh in us,

21 Unto him be glory in the church by Christ Jesus throughout all ages, world without end. Amen." (KJV)

This is the second great prayer of Paul in Ephesians. He is progressive in his prayers for the believers. In chapter one, he prayed that they would have their eyes enlightened so they could see and understand what God has already done for the believer. Now as he leads us into the next major phase—walk, Paul again prays.

1. Think about sitting and how much energy you expend. Now compare it to walking. There is a significantly greater amount of energy expended in walking. As you might expect, in Ephesians 3:16, Paul makes a key request of God. What is it?

_____

_____

_____

2. Without strength and might, we cannot walk and do the good works God has ordained for us. The word "might" in this passage is the same word for the power that raised Jesus Christ from the dead—resurrection power! This is what Paul wants God to give each of us. How and where does this occur?

_____

_____

_____

What is the inner man? Do you remember when Christ told Nicodemus that he must be born again? This is what happens when you invite Christ to come into your heart. He creates a new man inside of you—the inner man. This is where the Spirit of God resides and communicates with us.

3. Look at this passage in Titus 3:5. It describes the process of salvation. List what you find.

_____

_____

_____

The Holy Ghost is now alive or renewed within us again. Again? This refers to Adam, who originally had the Spirit as part of his being (body, soul, spirit). However, when he sinned, his nature was changed to be only body and soul. The spirit was disconnected or died. When God saves us, this proper relationship of body, soul, and spirit is restored.

4. For God to strengthen us with might in the inner man, it is not automatic. Look at Romans 8:5-14 and see if you can discover what God requires of us.

_____

_____

_____

Even though we have new life within us, God does not take away our free will—our ability to make choices. If we continue to pursue the things of our flesh (See Galatians 5:19-21), we walk back into death and cannot please God. However, if we choose to obey what the Spirit reveals, we find that the lusts of the flesh die out. Some die quickly and some take a long time to die—our war against the flesh never ends until Christ calls us home.

5. Paul continues in his prayer that Christ may dwell in your hearts by faith so that you would be rooted and ground in love. What do you think that means?

_____

_____

_____

6. The word "dwell" is also discussed in Colossians 3:16. If we let, choose or allow Christ to dwell within us, then certain attitudes and actions should occur. What are they?

_____

_____

_____

Are these the attitudes you have within your heart? Or is it grumbling, murmuring, and complaining?

7. Let the Word of God dwell in your heart is described in Joshua 1:8. Let me ask you two questions and write down your answers to them.

    a. "Do any of you want to be successful and prosperous in life?"

_____

_____

_____

    b. "Are you willing to do whatever it takes for that to become true in your life?" How would you answer these questions?

_____

_____

_____

8. Now look and see if you can discover God's process. God states that "if" you do something, then He promises to do something for you. Write down what He will do.

_____

_____

_____

God always makes our walk and blessing conditional. If you do things His way, then He is ever faithful to keep His promises to you. As we take God up on His offer, our faith grows stronger as we learn He is absolutely faithful to His Word. This is why we need to let God's Word dwell in our hearts and follow the leading of His Spirit.

The next two verses in Paul's prayer are intriguing. Having been strengthened with might in the inner man, having Christ dwell in our hearts by faith, rooted and grounded in love, Paul now asks that we:

Ephesians 3:18-19
"18 May be able to comprehend with all saints what is the breadth, and length, and depth, and height;
19 And to know the love of Christ, which passeth knowledge, that ye might be filled with all the fulness of God." (KJV)

These two verses speak to the walk of the believer. For each of us on our journey, we are constantly amazed at the love of Christ and the extent of His love. As we begin to comprehend and experience more fully the extent of Christ's love for us, God enables us to grow. As we accept and know by experience the love of Christ, then we become filled with more and more of God's divine nature.

The conclusion of Paul's second prayer is in Ephesians 3:20 and 21.

Ephesians 3:20-21
"20 Now unto him that is able to do exceeding abundantly above all that we ask or think, according to the power that worketh in us,

21 Unto him be glory in the church by Christ Jesus throughout all ages, world without end. Amen." (KJV)

9. God is able to do exceedingly and abundantly above all that we ask or even think. But some think this is a blank check to get anything we want, unlimited prosperity and wealth in this life. But God has conditions, the "if", followed by the "then" part. Look at James 4:1-4 and put down what you discover.

_____

_____

_____

God forbid that you would so lust after things of this world, which makes us God's enemy. Our motives for what we do are always important. It is vital to allow God to search our hearts and minds to see if we have wicked motives. He will give us an honest evaluation. Otherwise, we are very good at pulling a con job on ourselves.

Jeremiah 17:9-10
"9 The heart is deceitful above all things, and desperately wicked: who can know it?

10 I the LORD search the heart, I try the reins, even to give every man according to his ways, and according to the fruit of his doings." (KJV)

My prayer for each of us is that we would ask God to search our hearts and minds so that we do things that only please Him as expressed by the Psalmist.

Psalms 139:23-24
"23 Search me, O God, and know my heart: try me, and know my thoughts:
24 And see if there be any wicked way in me, and lead me in the way everlasting." (KJV)

May we each allow God to search our hearts, to cleanse them and then to lead us in His way, all to His glory.

Matthew 5:16 "Let your light so shine before men, that they may see your good works, and glorify your Father which is in heaven." (KJV)

Study 7: Walk Worthy of Your Calling
Ephesians 4:1-7

Ephesians 4:1-7

"1 I therefore, the prisoner of the Lord, beseech you that ye walk worthy of the vocation wherewith ye are called,

2 With all lowliness and meekness, with longsuffering, forbearing one another in love;

3 Endeavouring to keep the unity of the Spirit in the bond of peace.

4 There is one body, and one Spirit, even as ye are called in one hope of your calling;

5 One Lord, one faith, one baptism,

6 One God and Father of all, who is above all, and through all, and in you all.

7 But unto every one of us is given grace according to the measure of the gift of Christ." (KJV)

This study starts with the second reference to the key word—walk. In this short passage, Paul lays an important foundation to our walking worthy of who we are. Our attitude toward our Lord and other believers is of paramount importance. Paul begins by referring to himself as the prisoner of the Lord. The word for prisoner is bond-slave. In the Old Testament, an Israelite could voluntarily become a slave to another Israelite for up to seven years. Every seven years, all slave contracts were torn up and everyone was set free. However, if a servant wished to remain with his master, he could elect to do so. The master would then take an awl and pierce the servants' ear, which indicated he was a slave for life. Paul says he voluntarily became a bond-slave, a lifetime servant to the Lord. Based on his lifestyle and faithful service, he begs the new believers to walk worthy of the vocation into which they are called.

1. In Ephesians 4:2 and 3, Paul lists several key attitudes that should characterize our walk. List them.

_____

_____

_____

2. The first key attitude he mentions is "with all lowliness." Another word frequently used is with all humility. In Philippians 2:5-8, Paul outlines what true lowliness is through the example of Christ. Describe what you see in this passage.

_____

_____

_____

Jesus Christ Himself, even though he was every bit God, chose to make himself of no reputation. Whenever a guest speaker is introduced, a brief resume of their experience and qualifications are usually given. The intent is to convey to you that they are worth listening to. But Christ made Himself of no reputation so he could relate to the lowest of humanity—the publicans, sinners, and outcasts, not just the elite. The form He chose was that of a servant, not someone giving orders or commands. Instead Christ chose to obey God, even if it meant being crucified.

3. Look at Luke 22:42 and write down how Christ responded, even when He knew the crucifixion was about to happen.

_____

_____

_____

In Ephesians 4:2, Paul continues with "all lowliness and meekness." Meekness is a word commonly associated with wimp, pushover, or a coward. Yet that is far from what its biblical meaning is. Think of a large, powerful stallion. He has great speed and size and could easily maim or kill you. Its teeth can snap your arm in two. Yet, with a bridle and bit, this mighty animal is brought under control and taught to obey its riders' commands. Meekness is great might and power that is under control. In today's world, it is so easy to strike back, to get even, to make things right from your perspective, or to lash out with a verbal assault. Yet as a worthy believer, we keep those hot, hostile emotions and reactions in check. We allow the Holy Spirit to temper and direct our reactions to overcome and prevent such abuse.

4. This same meekness is closely related to the next attitude—longsuffering. This is not an attitude of suffering for the things we do wrong, but rather for the things we do right! Take a look at 1 Peter 2:19-23 and describe what you see in those verses.

_____

_____

_____

When we endure suffering, having done nothing wrong, we are following the example of Christ. He suffered greatly, even death on the cross. In today's world, the first response is to get even, to belittle the other person, to attack their character, to grumble and complain, or even file a lawsuit. Yet, Christ didn't twist facts to justify Himself or even prove His cause was just. He simply did not respond in kind, He did not threaten, but rather committed all His works unto God. He left the judgment in God's hands. Christ calls us to do likewise. Peter, after the Sanhedrin had warned him not to speak anymore in the name of Jesus, greatly rejoiced that he was considered worthy to suffer for His sake. Paul had a similar sentiment:

Philippians 3:10
"10 That I may know him, and the power of his resurrection, and the fellowship of his sufferings, being made conformable unto his death;" (KJV)

5. Paul was eager to become a partaker in the sufferings of Christ, even if it meant being conformed to His death. How does your attitude compare to that of Paul?

_____

_____

_____

Today, as long as it is convenient, we will follow Christ. But what if we face suffering when we do nothing wrong, and longsuffering at that (not short term but ongoing)? Many of us would say, "You must be kidding me. This is not what I expected being a Christian would be like." But that is exactly what Christ calls us to do, when we walk worthy of the vocation into which you are called. May God give each of us more of His power and Spirit so we may be able to endure with longsuffering when we have done nothing wrong.

6. The next phrase in Ephesians 4:2 is "forbearing one another in love." What do you think that means?

_____

_____

_____

7. This attitude is very important to walking worthy of Christ. Forbearing is very close to several concepts expressed in the Lord's Prayer in Matthew 6:9-15. See if you can discover what they are.

_____

_____

_____

8. The next phrase occurs in Ephesians 4:3 and is probably the hardest for us as believers to comply with, i.e., "endeavoring to keep the unity of the Spirit in the bond of peace." What in your opinion do you think it means?

_____

_____

_____

We must do everything within our power to cooperate with and allow the Spirit to create the unity and peace He desires among believers. Are you willing to allow the Spirit to change your mind and attitude? Do you really want only what God wants in a particular situation? Frequently, we are selfish and couch our prayers in pious sounding terms, but in reality, we want God to answer our prayer in accordance with our wishes.

9. Take a look and see if you can discover some of the underlying attitudes of why people fasted as found in Isaiah 58:1-4.

_____

_____

_____

10. Too frequently, our motives are wrong and focused on what we want. But look at Isaiah 58:5-8 and write down the attitudes that God says are important.

_____

_____

_____

May we yield our will in order to do what He wants. This will allow His Spirit to have free rein among all believers in the church, shaping it to glorify the Father. May each of us endeavor or really work hard to keep the unity of the Spirit in the bond of peace and thus walk worthy of the One who called us.

Now let's look at Ephesians 4:4-6. The word "one" occurs several times. The word "one" is also another word for unity. In Deuteronomy 6:4, Jewish prayers frequently open with, "Hear O Israel, the LORD our God is one LORD." (KJV). Yet, when we look at Matthew 3:16-17, we see the LORD is more than one entity—Father, Son, and Holy Ghost.

11. List the different aspects of oneness or unity found in Ephesians 4:4-6.

_____

_____

_____

Unity of the believers through common experience is God's will for each of us. Do not mistake unity as God making each of us with a cookie cutter mold. We are diverse, yet unified. Verse seven states that unto each of us is given grace according to the gift of Christ. As the passage in 1 Corinthians 12 indicated, the Spirit has given each one of us a measure of God's grace in order that it is used to maintain and nurture His multi-faceted unity. Walk worthy of that grace.

Study 8: Walk in the Body of Christ—The Church
Ephesians 4:8-16

Ephesians 4:8-16

"8 Wherefore he saith, When he ascended up on high, he led captivity captive, and gave gifts unto men.

9 (Now that he ascended, what is it but that he also descended first into the lower parts of the earth?

10 He that descended is the same also that ascended up far above all heavens, that he might fill all things.)

11 And he gave some, apostles; and some, prophets; and some, evangelists; and some, pastors and teachers;

12 For the perfecting of the saints, for the work of the ministry, for the edifying of the body of Christ:

13 Till we all come in the unity of the faith, and of the knowledge of the Son of God, unto a perfect man, unto the measure of the stature of the fulness of Christ:

14 That we henceforth be no more children, tossed to and fro, and carried about with every wind of doctrine, by the sleight of men, and cunning craftiness, whereby they lie in wait to deceive;

15 But speaking the truth in love, may grow up into him in all things, which is the head, even Christ:

16 From whom the whole body fitly joined together and compacted by that which every joint supplieth, according to the effectual working in the measure of every part, maketh increase of the body unto the edifying of itself in love." (KJV)

In calling us to walk worthy and in unity, God always provides a way for this to happen. His chosen vehicle to make the walk in unity feasible is the church or body of Christ. God does not call us to walk alone but rather in mutual dependence on each other. From verse ten we learn that to start this body, Christ gave men with special gifts—apostles, prophets, evangelists, pastors, and teachers. Each fulfilled a unique role in the early, embryonic stages of the church.

1. According to Ephesians 4:12, Christ gave gifted people for three main purposes. What are they?

_____

_____

_____

2. Ephesians 4:13 reveals the end objectives of the edifying work listed in verse 12—to be unified in two areas. What are they?

_____

_____

_____

Ephesians 4:13 then talks about the yardstick of how well we are doing in our faith. When I was a child, my parents would put a mark on the wall so I could see how much I had grown. It is the same concept with our faith—always growing taller. But we must measure it only against the stature of the fullness of Christ. You see, as children, we start comparing ourselves against others.

3. In John 21:18-22, Jesus had just told Peter how he was going to die. But Peter gazed at John and said, "What about him?" How did Jesus respond?

_____

_____

_____

4. Ephesians 4:14-15 continues the discussion on growing toward maturity. It talks about children and how they react to what they hear and see. What do these verses describe?

_____

_____

_____

5. We are told to "be no more children." As you observe children interacting, you will notice that they have an unusual propensity to say mean and hurtful things—you're dumb, you're ugly, you're fat, you're slow, you must be a retard, etc. Ephesians 4:15 then describes what must take place to move us beyond childish ways. What does it say?

_____

_____

_____

Another way of "speaking the truth in love" is described later in Ephesians. It is to only say things that will build up someone, not tear them down. This kind of speech can only come from our reliance on the Holy Spirit to guard our tongues. Look at how James puts it in his epistle.

James 3:16-18
"16 For where envying and strife is, there is confusion and every evil work.
17 But the wisdom that is from above is first pure, then peaceable, gentle, and easy to be intreated, full of mercy and good fruits, without partiality, and without hypocrisy.
18 And the fruit of righteousness is sown in peace of them that make peace."(KJV)

6. When we allow the wisdom of God through the Spirit to have control according to the passage in James, how is that described?

_____

_____

_____

7. Having learned to speak the truth in love, we continue to grow to maturity. In Ephesians 4:16, we find the phrase: "maketh increase of the body unto the edifying of itself in love." How do you think that can happen?

_____

_____

_____

If the body is to be fully functional, then each part has to fulfill its role. Consider what Paul says in Corinthians.

1 Corinthians 12:14-18
"14 For the body is not one member, but many.
15 If the foot shall say, Because I am not the hand, I am not of the body; is it therefore not of the body?
16 And if the ear shall say, Because I am not the eye, I am not of the body; is it therefore not of the body?
17 If the whole body were an eye, where were the hearing? If the whole were hearing, where were the smelling?
18 But now hath God set the members every one of them in the body, as it hath pleased him."
(KJV)

Again, everyone must do their part. Take a team sport like football. For a runner to make a touchdown, every other player on his team must execute their assignment properly. If some deliberately misses a block, the runner goes nowhere. But when everyone does their part, a touchdown results. The ability of the body to grow is based on the same principle. If someone decides they do not want to participate with the rest of the body, then the whole body is impacted.

8. Another illustration I like is that of a bonfire. With a bonfire, you may have a large group of logs burning together with flames shooting up thirty feet or more. Each log is blazing in flames and red hot. But what happens if you pull one of those logs out of the fire and set if off by itself?

_____

_____

_____

Initially, the log still has flames shooting off of it. But soon those flames die off and you still see red embers in the log. A short while later, all you see is smoke as the embers die out. Finally, you have a charred log that has no fire coming from it at all. This is what happens to believers who do not want to fulfill their role in the growth of the church. They become scarred, cold, and do not fulfill their God-given purpose—shipwrecked and castaway.

I'd like to make one final point about the absolute necessity of staying connected to and walking in the body. National Geographic has a TV film about zebras and crocodiles. The zebras must cross a river to go from their summer pasture to their winter feeding area. The herd of about 300 zebras must cross the river, but they know the crocodiles are there. In fact, there are normally only about three or four crocodiles at this river crossing, but now there are over 50. The crocodiles know it is harvest time too. Finally, the zebras get up enough courage and the entire herd of 300 stampedes into the river together. Then you see the crocodiles go into action. They are snapping and grabbing the zebras. Finally, the fighting in the water subsides.

9. How many zebras do you think made it to the other side: fifty, a hundred, two hundred?

_____

_____

_____

In fact, all 300 made it across the river. Because they went together, the crocodiles did not kill one single zebra. The crocodiles would have hold of one zebra and another would go running by, so they would let go of the one and go after the other. As a result the 300 zebras made it across successfully, although many had scrapes and bleeding cuts. However, the crocodiles went hungry.

But after the main herd has crossed the river, the TV shows a lone male zebra prancing by himself. He is a stud and does not need to go when everyone else goes. Finally, he decides to start out into the river to cross and catch up to the rest of the herd. How do you think he did? He did not even get 20 feet into the river before he became a meal.

You see, God has put the body, the church, together for many reasons, the foremost of which is safety. As we each fulfill the role God has given us, the church continues as a place of safety and growth. The church builds itself up because of the care and love we have for each other.

Study 9: Walk in Newness of Life

Ephesians 4:17-32

Ephesians 4:17-32

"17 This I say therefore, and testify in the Lord, that ye henceforth walk not as other Gentiles walk, in the vanity of their mind,

18 Having the understanding darkened, being alienated from the life of God through the ignorance that is in them, because of the blindness of their heart:

19 Who being past feeling have given themselves over unto lasciviousness, to work all uncleanness with greediness.

20 But ye have not so learned Christ;

21 If so be that ye have heard him, and have been taught by him, as the truth is in Jesus:

22 That ye put off concerning the former conversation the old man, which is corrupt according to the deceitful lusts;

23 And be renewed in the spirit of your mind;

24 And that ye put on the new man, which after God is created in righteousness and true holiness.

25 Wherefore putting away lying, speak every man truth with his neighbour: for we are members one of another.

26 Be ye angry, and sin not: let not the sun go down upon your wrath:

27 Neither give place to the devil.

28 Let him that stole steal no more: but rather let him labour, working with his hands the thing which is good, that he may have to give to him that needeth.

29 Let no corrupt communication proceed out of your mouth, but that which is good to the use of edifying, that it may minister grace unto the hearers.

30 And grieve not the holy Spirit of God, whereby ye are sealed unto the day of redemption.

31 Let all bitterness, and wrath, and anger, and clamour, and evil speaking, be put away from you, with all malice:

32 And be ye kind one to another, tenderhearted, forgiving one another, even as God for Christ's sake hath forgiven you." (KJV)

Paul begins this section by contrasting the old way of living with how our new life in Christ is to be different. We are not to walk the same way we used to. Ephesians 4:17-19 describe the various conditions of the lost.

1. List the characteristics from these verses. Were any of them applicable to you?

_____

_____

_____

Most unsaved people walk in the vanity of their mind, deceived into thinking they are the ultimate authority in determining what is right for their lives. Consequently, they reject the truth about their sinful condition. I have listed several passages for you to review and discuss.

2. Write down the key points you find in Matthew 13:3-4, 18-19.

_____

_____

_____

3. Write down the key points you find in 2 Corinthians 4:3-4.

_____

_____

_____

4. List the five most important things you see in Romans 1:21-32.

_____

_____

_____

5. Now let's look at Ephesians 4:20-21, where Paul says these kinds of bad behavior should not be part of our lives "if" we are Christians. How do you know if you are a Christian according to these verses?

_____

_____

_____

Next in Ephesians 4:22-24, Paul uses the analogy of putting off one way of living and putting on a new way of life. When you have gotten really dirty working in the yard, what do you do before going out to a movie with friends? You put off the dirty clothes, take a hot shower and get cleaned up. You then put on some nice cologne or perfume and put on clean clothes. That is the process Paul is trying to communicate.

6. A key component of putting on a new way of life is described as being renewed in the spirit of your mind. What do you think it means?

_____

_____

_____

7. Remember Paul prayed for enlightenment that our minds would be able to comprehend the new things of God. The Spirit of God brings this renewal at the time of our new birth (see Titus 3:5). Another aspect of this renewal in our minds is found in Romans 12:1-2. Describe what you see in these verses.

_____

_____

_____

8. Next, look at Ephesians 4:25-29. Paul begins to outline some of the things we must put off and some of the things we must put on.

    a.   List the things to put off.

_____

_____

_____

    b.   List the things to put on.

_____

_____

_____

9. I want us to take some time to look at Ephesians 4:26-27, which deals with anger and whether or not it leads to sin. Is getting angry a sin? Explain your answer.

_____

_____

_____

Anger becomes a sin if it is not dealt with before the sun goes down. I take that to mean that whatever caused you to be angry must be settled or at least the process of reaching a settlement must begin within 24 hours. For example, you get angry at your wife because she did not fix dinner. She said she was too tired after her playing cards with the ladies at the club that afternoon. If you brush it off and stomp out the door to go get a meal at a restaurant, you have not dealt with your anger. If you ignore it, the anger begins to fester into resentment toward your wife and your love for her may start growing cold. Instead you need to have a discussion with her within 24 hours to clear the air. When you do, sin is turned away from your door and the devil loses his opportunity to split you apart.

10. There are many other negative consequences of anger that is not dealt with properly. What are some of the negative, hurtful things that happened to you because of anger? You may also list hurtful things you did to others because of your anger.

_____

_____

_____

11. In Ephesians 4:28, Paul says if you are a thief, steal no more. What is the behavior we should put on and why?

_____

_____

_____

12. In Ephesians 4:29, Paul says to let no corrupt communication proceed out of your mouth. What do you think it means? List several examples you have or are currently dealing with.

_____

_____

_____

13. Then Paul talks about our relationship with the Holy Spirit in Ephesians 4:30-32. There are things we can do that grieve or cause sorrow and tears to God's Holy Spirit. Describe what you find that would grieve the Holy Spirit from these verses.

_____

_____

_____

14. By contrast, someone under the control of the Holy Spirit acts a certain way. List what you find.

_____

_____

_____

You see, the Holy Spirit never causes us to do any of the evil things, but our evil nature does. We must put off these behaviors and nail them to the cross. That is why Paul prayed in chapter three that God would give you strength and power in the inner man by the Holy Spirit.

Look at the process found in Romans 8:12-17. As we learn to listen to and obey the leading of the Holy Spirit, the fleshly desires die out. This will also confirm to us that our faith is real, that we are indeed His adopted children. Yes, it will be hard, because our flesh and its lusts never go completely away. But thanks be to God that He gives us His new life and power so we are free to obey His leading.

Study 10: Walk in Love

Ephesians 5:1-7

Ephesians 5:1-7
"1   Be ye therefore followers of God, as dear children;
2   And walk in love, as Christ also hath loved us, and hath given himself for us an offering and a sacrifice to God for a sweetsmelling savour.
3   But fornication, and all uncleanness, or covetousness, let it not be once named among you, as becometh saints;
4   Neither filthiness, nor foolish talking, nor jesting, which are not convenient: but rather giving of thanks.
5   For this ye know, that no whoremonger, nor unclean person, nor covetous man, who is an idolater, hath any inheritance in the kingdom of Christ and of God.
6   Let no man deceive you with vain words: for because of these things cometh the wrath of God upon the children of disobedience.
7   Be not ye therefore partakers with them." (KJV)

Chapter five begins a marvelous section of application in our walk with Christ. Please notice that Paul calls us "dear children", which is an indicator of where this passage fits in our spiritual journey to full maturity in Christ. Paul outlines three key aspects of our walk if we are to be followers of God: love, light, and circumspectly redeeming the time. In this study, we will examine the first one—walk in love.

The first area we want to examine occurs in verse 3. Our walk as dear children is to walk in love as Christ walked, i.e., follow His example. Jesus loved us so much that He sacrificed Himself as the Lamb of God on the cross, which is then described as a sweet-smelling fragrance. We too are to be a sweet-smelling fragrance. You see, as we walk in love the way Christ wants us to walk, we produce body odor. Body odor? Yes, it is like the kind that comes when we sweat and toil at work. To those who are saved, it is a sweet fragrance unto life. But to those who are lost, it is a repulsive odor of death.

2 Corinthians 2:14-16a
"14 Now thanks be unto God, which always causeth us to triumph in Christ, and maketh manifest the savour of his knowledge by us in every place.
15 For we are unto God a sweet savour of Christ, in them that are saved, and in them that perish:
16 To the one we are the savour of death unto death; and to the other the savour of life unto life. . . ." (KJV)

1. When we walk in love, we are a very positive witness without ever having said one word. Now let me ask you, "What kind of body odor does your walk produce?"

_____

_____

_____

2. By contrast, Paul gives us indicators of the things that will really make us "stink of death" in Ephesians 5:3-5. List what you find.

_____

_____

_____

This is a pretty interesting list. Fornication is sexual sin outside of marriage (adultery in marriage). It includes fantasizing having sex with other women, which is another word for pornography. Christ put it this way:

Matthew 5:27-28
"27 Ye have heard that it was said by them of old time, Thou shalt not commit adultery:
28 But I say unto you, That whosoever looketh on a woman to lust after her hath committed adultery with her already in his heart." (KJV)

3. The next phrase in Ephesians 5:3, "all uncleanness" is a very inclusive term. What areas in your life could be subject to uncleanness?

_____

_____

_____

It applies to deeds and thoughts. Here are a few words that may help: defiled, dirty, filthy, tainted, impure, corrupted, compromised, and contaminated. All of these things pertain to how our garments and the fragrance of our lives appear to God.

4. In the church at Corinth (see 1 Corinthians 5:1-8), a man had committed a grievous sin of having sex with his father's wife. And everyone in the church knew about it. Rather than mourning over this sin, how did the church deal with it?

_____

_____

_____

Paul had a much different view in 1 Corinthians 5:6-8. He uses the analogy of leaven to describe their attitude. Leaven in the Old Testament was identified with the Passover event when God set His people free from the slavery of Egypt. Most bread today is very fluffy and light, because a little yeast or leaven is added to the bread dough before it is baked. The yeast, which is actually a form of bacteria, ferments and puts off gas. The gas causes the bread to rise as it is baking. By contrast, bread without yeast is like a flat tortilla.

5. As you look at 1 Corinthians 5:6-8, what does Paul instruct the church to do?

_____

_____

_____

Contamination from leaven was reflected in God's command about who you could marry. God continually told His people to remain separate from the other people of the land, not to intermarry. God knew that the Gentile women would corrupt their husbands and cause them to worship false gods (see Deuteronomy 7:3-4). And it happened to the wisest man on earth, Solomon, so don't think it cannot happen to you (see 1 Kings 11:1, 4-5).

6. Look at Jude 1:20-23. There is one interesting item about uncleanness there. See if you can discover what it is.

_____

_____

_____

7. Uncleanness in our life may also be due to blindness in how we see things. Look at Revelation 3:15-19. What are the attitudes of uncleanness you find there?

_____

_____

_____

8. Christ had a very severe warning for the church at Laodicea in Revelation 3:15-19. Because you are lukewarm, I (Christ) will vomit you out of heaven. Lukewarm means half-hearted effort, straddling the fence. I can follow Christ when it is convenient or the world when it suits me. But what did Christ tell them they needed to do?

_____

_____

_____

Then Paul in Ephesians 5:3 gives one last thing we do not want on our resume: covetousness. It means I want something other than what I have with a very strong desire. It is the roaming eye looking for something I do not have—a prettier wife, a flashier car, a bigger house, a better paying job, praise from people (rather than God), et cetera.

9. Paul really puts it in perspective in 1 Timothy 6:6-11. Put down what you find.

_____

_____

_____

Covetousness is primarily an attitude of discontentment with God and what He has given me. Rather than focusing on the blessing the Creator wishes to bestow on us, we focus on other things. And there is great risk—pierced with many sorrows, if we allow our lust for wealth and things to dominate. The Israelites demanded meat. They were tired of manna. So God sent them quail, but it caused great harm to their spiritual being.

Psalms 106:13-15
"13 They soon forgat his works; they waited not for his counsel:
14 But lusted exceedingly in the wilderness, and tempted God in the desert.
15 And he gave them their request; but sent leanness into their soul." (KJV)

The final three items mentioned in Ephesians 5:4 by Paul all pertain to what comes out of our mouth—filthy talk; foolish, empty, or boastful talk; and untimely jokes. You see, what comes out of our mouth is the biggest indication of what is going on in our heart.

10. Look at Matthew 12:34-37 and list what you find.

_____

_____

_____

Every idle word you and I speak, we will have to give account thereof in the judgment day. Be aware too, everyone else will be listening in on your explanation. It is like having your conversation with God on live TV and broadcast worldwide. And everyone is tuned in!

Paul concludes Ephesians 5:4 by giving what is acceptable to God. Rather than trash talk, let your life and words reflect an attitude of thanksgiving. You see, when we give thanks, it means we are glad for where we are and how God has provided for us.

11. When we give thanks, it also carries a sweet promise from God found in Philippians 4:6-7. See if you can discover what it is.

_____

_____

_____

Please note that we are not to be anxious or worried about anything. Anything? Yes, that means anything. Next we must give thanks in everything. Well, in prison that can be a real challenge, but God means everything. When we do what Philippians 4:6 says, then we will have God's peace in our hearts and life. Have you ever had trouble going to sleep because something is on your mind? Or you may not even be aware of anything, but you still cannot sleep. If so, ask God to reveal whatever you are anxious about or if there is any area that you are not giving thanks in. When He does (and He will), reapply Philippians 4:6 and see what happens. I have always found a sweet, deep peace and rest afterward.

12. Now, let's turn our attention to Ephesians 5:5-7. Verse five is very severe. No one who is a whoremonger, an unclean person, a covetous person or idolater has any inheritance in the kingdom of Christ and of God. Well, some of us have been involved in those very sins. Therefore, does it mean I am not or cannot be saved? How would you answer that question?

_____

_____

_____

In Corinthians, Paul gives us a better explanation.

1 Corinthians 6:9-11
"9 Know ye not that the unrighteous shall not inherit the kingdom of God? Be not deceived: neither fornicators, nor idolaters, nor adulterers, nor effeminate, nor abusers of themselves with mankind,

10 Nor thieves, nor covetous, nor drunkards, nor revilers, nor extortioners, shall inherit the kingdom of God.

11 And such were some of you: but ye are washed, but ye are sanctified, but ye are justified in the name of the Lord Jesus, and by the Spirit of our God." (KJV)

Notice 1 Corinthians 6:11: "and such were some of you, but now you are washed, sanctified, and justified in Jesus name and confirmed by the Holy Spirit of God." All of us are sinners. But God has redeemed us and given us a new purpose.

But if we continue to reject God's leading and chastisement in order to continue in our sinful ways, then we are walking a very dangerous line. Is your faith genuine or just empty words? True faith always compels us to act in a manner pleasing to God. We can say we are saved, but if we continue to frequent prostitutes or continue to steal repeatedly, then our faith may be phony. God calls us to righteous living, a walk that is worthy of our calling, and one in God-like love.

Do not be deceived by vain words. Some think, "I've never been involved in those types of evil activities. My following Christ and calling on His name must mean that I'm alright." People like that had an exchange with Christ in Matthew 7:21-27. Let's take a look at it.

13. What things did these people list as part of their accomplishments in Matthew 7:22?

_____

_____

_____

14. How did Christ react to them in Matthew 7:23?

_____

_____

_____

Matthew 7:24 to 27 give us an illustration of the importance of hearing the word <u>and</u> doing what it says. Notice, being obedient does not exempt us from the storms of life. They will come upon each one of us. But we survive the storms because of our foundation or connection to Christ, the abiding in Him spoken of in John 15:5. But notice what happens to the one who hears but does <u>not</u> obey? When the storm came, it collapsed the house—a great and terrible loss.

Finally, in Ephesians 5:6-7, Paul describes the end result of such evil conduct—the wrath of God is poured out on the "children of disobedience." I believe this means those who continually, persistently, and habitually disobey and mock the righteousness of God. Just like what we looked at earlier in Psalms chapter one, do not partake of their deceitful works.

Psalms 1:1-3
"1 Blessed is the man that walketh not in the counsel of the ungodly, nor standeth in the way of sinners, nor sitteth in the seat of the scornful.
2 But his delight is in the law of the LORD; and in his law doth he meditate day and night.
3 And he shall be like a tree planted by the rivers of water, that bringeth forth his fruit in his season; his leaf also shall not wither; and whatsoever he doeth shall prosper." (KJV)

Study 11: Walk as Light and Circumspectly, Redeeming the Time

Ephesians 5:8-16

Ephesians 5:8-16

"8 For ye were sometimes darkness, but now are ye light in the Lord: walk as children of light:

9 (For the fruit of the Spirit is in all goodness and righteousness and truth;)

10 Proving what is acceptable unto the Lord.

11 And have no fellowship with the unfruitful works of darkness, but rather reprove them.

12 For it is a shame even to speak of those things which are done of them in secret.

13 But all things that are reproved are made manifest by the light: for whatsoever doth make manifest is light.

14 Wherefore he saith, Awake thou that sleepest, and arise from the dead, and Christ shall give thee light.

15 See then that ye walk circumspectly, not as fools, but as wise,

16 Redeeming the time, because the days are evil." (KJV)

In chapter five, Paul outlines the three key aspects of our walk if we are to be followers of God: love, light, and circumspectly redeeming the time. In the previous study, we looked at walking in love. In this study, we will examine the last two—walk in light and circumspectly redeeming the time.

1. Paul starts his discussion of light by looking at what is its opposite—darkness. Before we knew Christ, we were trapped in darkness. List some of the emotions you felt when you walked in darkness.

_____

_____

_____

2. Now let's look at what light does. List as many things as you can think of.

_____

_____

_____

3. Paul reminds us that when we walk as children of light, we produce several kinds of fruit. What are they?

_____

_____

_____

4. In Ephesians 5:10, Paul challenges us to prove what is acceptable to the Lord. You see God does not want us to react in blind faith, but rather He challenges us to put Him to the test. Look at Malachi 3:10 and Romans 12:1-2 and list what you find.

_____

_____

_____

5. What makes proving what is acceptable to the Lord difficult is that we often do not do it exactly the way God said to do it. In 1 Samuel 15, Saul was given some very specific instructions: kill all of the Amalekites and all they possessed, whether material things or herds. All was to be destroyed. How did Saul do in following everything that he was instructed to do?

_____

_____

_____

6. But Saul only partially obeyed and the results were disastrous. Read 1 Samuel 15:19-23 and list the results of his partial obedience.

_____

_____

_____

Please note 1 Samuel 15:22-23. God is not interested in our religious actions, but rather in our full obedience to whatever He has commanded. Saul's 95% obedience was characterized as rebellion, witchcraft (practicing witchcraft was a capital offense), stubbornness, iniquity and idolatry. Our partial obedience is rejecting the word of God.

7. God challenges each of us to do things His way in complete 100% obedience. Then God says to watch and see what the results are. When you put Him to the test and do it His way, what are the results according to Romans 12:2?

_____

_____

_____

8. Another aspect of walking as children of light is found in 1 John 1:5-7. Put down what you find.

_____

_____

_____

God calls us to walk in the light as He is in the light. This enables us to have true fellowship with Christ and each other. Are you willing to have the spotlight of God shine on your life and see if there is any darkness in you? If we are to have true communion and fellowship with God and each other, then known sin must be dealt with through the blood of Jesus Christ.

9. But how do I know if there is sin in my life? Look at Psalms 139:23-24 and write down what you see.

_____

_____

_____

Simply ask God to use His searchlight on your heart to reveal if there is anything offensive to Him. Then listen to what the Spirit reveals and brings to your mind. Then you must confess it, forsake it, and forget it.

10. Why do we do it this way rather than serious soul searching or introspection? Look at Jeremiah 17:9-10 and uncover the reasons.

_____

_____

_____

As we walk as children of light, Paul goes on to say that we should not fellowship or participate in the unfruitful works of darkness (which we partook of before). Instead, we are to reprove them by our right living.

11. Because we give off light, people react to us in one of two ways. Look at John 3:19-21. What are the two ways?

_____

_____

_____

If people's deeds are evil, they will run from the light so they can hide in the darkness. Those who are attracted by the light want all to know that their deeds are true and a result of God's workmanship in their life. Just as we talked about body odor in a previous study, His light in us repels or attracts.

12. Another aspect of walking as children of light is found in Matthew 5:14-16. After reading it, how would you answer these questions, "How bright is your light shining for Christ?" and "What can keep you from shining brightly?"

_____

_____

_____

13. Most of us know 1 John 1:9, but do you know what Proverbs 28:13 tells us? Look at that verse and see what it adds to the principles found in 1 John 1:9.

_____

_____

_____

All of our walking as children of light helps to awakening people from sleep. That is what light does. We sleep soundly in a dark room, yet when the sun comes up, what happens? It lets our bodies know it is time to get up. We are the sunrise to those around us. God uses us to wake them up out of their dark sleep, so the light of Christ may shine in their hearts and give them life.

Walk Circumspectly

As a result of all of those verses, Paul tells us in Ephesians 5:15 one key characteristic of our walk—to walk circumspectly, not foolishly, but as wise. The word circumspectly is one of those $25 words, not in common use today. It means to be very careful and consider all of the possible consequences.

Let's look at a simple example. It is dark outside and you are late for supper. If you take a shortcut across the cow field, you might get home on time. But you forgot your flashlight. Should you take the shortcut? If you do, what do you think might happen? Yes, you stand a good chance of stepping on a cow pie (cow poop) and you will get in even more trouble if you walk inside with that on your shoes. Rather than chance it, you may have to walk or run around the field. There are lots of traps out there the enemy will use to ensnare you. We need His light and wisdom to avoid them or, if required, to flee from them.

14. James 3:13-18 gives us a contrast of Godly wisdom versus earthly or human wisdom. Put down what you find.

   a. Earthly wisdom

_____

_____

_____

b. Godly wisdom

_____

_____

_____

Redeem the Time

The final admonition of this study in Ephesians 5:16 is to redeem the time because the days are evil. Redeem the time, what is Paul getting at? Redeem means to buy back. If you pawn your car title or your watch, in order to get it back you must redeem it by paying an agreed upon sum of money. Christ did that for us when He redeemed us. We were sold as slaves of sin, slaves of the darkness. But Christ went into the darkness and deliberately purchased us. But why would the spotless Lamb of God buy you and me in the slave market? He did it in order to set us free from the slavery of sin so we might have the opportunity to choose to become slaves to righteousness (see Romans 6 through 8).

15. So how are we to buy back time? How can we reclaim yesterday or even an hour we have wasted slumbering? We cannot. So what is Paul's point?

_____

_____

_____

Focus on the time that you do have and make the most of what time we do have. We want our time to count for God and His glory. Remember, your time on this earth is short.

James 4:14
"14 Whereas ye know not what shall be on the morrow. For what is your life? It is even a vapour, that appeareth for a little time, and then vanisheth away." (KJV)

Christ reminded us also in Matthew's gospel to focus just on today.

Matthew 6:33-34
"33 But seek ye first the kingdom of God, and his righteousness; and all these things shall be added unto you.
34 Take therefore no thought for the morrow: for the morrow shall take thought for the things of itself. Sufficient unto the day is the evil thereof." (KJV)

May each of us walk as children of light, circumspectly as wise children, who redeem their time each day in order to bring all of the glory to God.

Study 12: Walk Filled by the Spirit
Ephesians 5:17-20

Ephesians 5:17-20

"17 Wherefore be ye not unwise, but understanding what the will of the Lord is.

18 And be not drunk with wine, wherein is excess; but be filled with the Spirit;

19 Speaking to yourselves in psalms and hymns and spiritual songs, singing and making melody in your heart to the Lord;

20 Giving thanks always for all things unto God and the Father in the name of our Lord Jesus Christ;" (KJV)

Whenever you see a passage begin with the word "Wherefore," then you need to pause and ask, "What is it there for?" Everything Paul has said previously has bearing on what he is about to reveal. He has just concluded with three aspects of our walk in Christ as His children: walk in love, walk as light, and walk circumspectly redeeming the time.

Practically speaking, how do we walk that way? Part of it comes from Paul's prayer in Ephesians 3:16. "That he would grant you, according to the riches of his glory, to be strengthened with might by his Spirit in the inner man;" (KJV)

You see, Paul knew we require strength and power by His Spirit in the inner man if we are to walk in love, to walk as light, and to walk circumspectly redeeming the time. Now Paul is going to reveal a critical key to our ability to walk properly.

1. Look at Ephesians 5:18 and see if you can discover what it is.

_____

_____

_____

2. He starts off by telling us not to get drunk with wine. What happens when you drink too much wine or other alcoholic beverages?

_____

_____

_____

3. Instead of being controlled by wine, Paul tells us to be filled with the Spirit. That is God's will for each of His children. So how do I get filled with the Spirit?

_____

_____

_____

If you look carefully at what Paul said, "Be filled with the Spirit", it is actually a command. Another way of looking at it is to consider a five gallon water jug. If you fill it with rocks and pebbles before you pour the water in, how many gallons of water will be in the container? Maybe, it will hold one or two gallons at most. When people go to drink, the water is dirty and it quickly runs out. In fact, a small pebble can clog the opening so only a trickle of water gets out. But that is not what God wants for us. Jesus in John's gospel said rivers of living water were to come out of lives.

John 7:38-39

"38 He that believeth on me, as the scripture hath said, out of his belly shall flow rivers of living water.

39 (But this spake he of the Spirit, which they that believe on him should receive: for the Holy Ghost was not yet given; because that Jesus was not yet glorified.)" (KJV)

Notice it did not say trickles, small streams, or even a river of living water would come out. But rather, we are to have <u>rivers</u> (more than one river, a super overabundance) of living water flowing from us.

4. What keeps us from having rivers of living water flowing from us?

_____

_____

_____

If you look at the jug, the rocks and pebbles in the water container represent sin in our lives. If we allow our fleshly desires to fill up the jug or our unforgiveness, then God cannot put very much of His living water in us. However, as we allow God to remove the rocks and pebbles, then we can hold more of His Spirit.

The big rocks are sometimes the easiest thing to remove. It is the little pebbles that can clog up the outpouring of His living water. Even a small known sin—backbiting, envy, murmuring, and the like can seriously inhibit God's ability to use you to minister to those He brings your way. You see, the living water is not just for us to consume, but for the thirsty, dying, and lost people around us who are trapped and enslaved by their sins. They long for water that truly satisfies, cleanses them of their sins, and gives them an eternal hope. As we allow God's Holy Spirit to fill our lives, the rivers of living water, a great overflowing stream, will change the desert around us into a bountiful and beautiful garden of life.

5. As we receive the Holy Ghost, He begins leading us in a process called "pruning." Look at John 15:1-5 and write down what you learn about this process.

_____

_____

_____

6. Another key aspect of this process is found in Psalms 139:23-24. What additional information does it reveal?

_____

_____

_____

7. Once you have allowed the Spirit to search your heart and you have confessed and agreed to forsake the sins He revealed, are there other ways of knowing if you are staying filled with the Spirit? Paul gives us a great spiritual thermometer as to whether or not we are filled with the Spirit in Ephesians 5:19-20. Write down what you find.

_____

_____

_____

8. In the last half of Ephesians 5:19, Paul talks about what is going on in our hearts. Describe what is going on in your heart right now. Is it a song of joy, fear, anxiety, anger or what?

_____

_____

_____

9. If we allow the Holy Spirit to fill our hearts, then there will be a beautiful melody of rejoicing going on. Look at Paul and Silas after they had been attacked and beaten and were then thrown into the deepest hole in prison in Acts 16:22-25. What was their attitude and response?

_____

_____

_____

Did you catch what their attitude was after having been stripped and beaten and put in shackles in the deep, darkest part of a prison? They were praying and singing praises to God. Is that the kind of melody going on in your life, especially in prison? If the melody is sour, off key, or non-existent, then you are not yet filled with the Spirit.

A lot of our heart response reflects our attitude toward God. Is He really in control of my life? Can I trust His promises? Take a look at Joseph in the Old Testament (Genesis chapters 37 through 45). He was sold into slavery by his jealous brothers. He became the head steward or manager in a rich household, only to be falsely accused of trying to rape the owner's wife. He was sent to jail and yet the scripture never records him griping at God. Because of his positive attitude, he is put in charge of all the prisoners.

10. Yet, all of this evil befell this man who had done no wrong. But God had other plans for his life. Years later, when he confronted his brothers and could have exacted revenge, in Genesis 45:4-8, God revealed His purpose to Joseph in all his trials. Write down what you think it was.

_____

_____

_____

11. Despite all of the adversities, Joseph never grumbled or griped at where he was. God had a purpose and plan for his life, which is what Paul is getting at in Ephesians 5:20. Look at that verse and tell me, "What is your reaction to it?"

_____

_____

_____

12. Despite all of our circumstances, the one who is filled by the Spirit will give thanks <u>in all things</u>. Paul gives us a great perspective on why we can give thanks in all things in Romans 8:28-39. Which ones impress you the most?

_____

_____

_____

All of these verses give us an indicator of whether or not we are filled with the Spirit, and to what level. Allow God to search your heart. Ask Him to reveal to you anything in your life that is keeping you from being filled with the Holy Spirit. We are told to take up our cross each day. In the same fashion, we must ask daily to be filled (and re-filled) with the Holy Spirit. This will empower us to walk in love, to walk in light, and to walk circumspectly redeeming the time. The constant filling and re-filling will allow rivers of living water to flow from our lives to meet the needs of a hurting and dying world of people all around us.

13. Walk is the second process of Sit-Walk-Stand. Think back over studies four through twelve and summarize the things required to "walk" on this page and the next. Include any key areas you feel God wants you to work on.

_____

_____

_____

_____

_____

_____

Study 13: Building Strong Marriage Foundations (Part 1)

Ephesians 5:21-33

Ephesians 5:21-33

"21 Submitting yourselves one to another in the fear of God.

22 Wives, submit yourselves unto your own husbands, as unto the Lord.

23 For the husband is the head of the wife, even as Christ is the head of the church: and he is the saviour of the body.

24 Therefore as the church is subject unto Christ, so let the wives be to their own husbands in every thing.

25 Husbands, love your wives, even as Christ also loved the church, and gave himself for it;

26 That he might sanctify and cleanse it with the washing of water by the word,

27 That he might present it to himself a glorious church, not having spot, or wrinkle, or any such thing; but that it should be holy and without blemish.

28 So ought men to love their wives as their own bodies. He that loveth his wife loveth himself.

29 For no man ever yet hated his own flesh; but nourisheth and cherisheth it, even as the Lord the church:

30 For we are members of his body, of his flesh, and of his bones.

31 For this cause shall a man leave his father and mother, and shall be joined unto his wife, and they two shall be one flesh.

32 This is a great mystery: but I speak concerning Christ and the church.

33 Nevertheless let every one of you in particular so love his wife even as himself; and the wife see that she reverence her husband." (KJV)

In our previous study, Paul laid the groundwork for what is required in this next section, which is devoted to relationships. Relationships can only develop properly when each believer is filled with and controlled by the Spirit. In this passage, Paul addresses the necessity of submitting to one another and how the roles for husbands and wives are to be lived.

Submitting to One Another

The first and most important set of relationships is our ability to be in submission to one another in the fear of God. Can you submit to each of your brothers or sisters here? You may say, "To some I can, but all?" Yes, all. You see, our submission to each other is based upon our fear of God. Our ultimate submission is to God. We don't worry about who is the chief or who is lower on the totem pole.

1. The disciples, in Matthew 20:26-28, were arguing over just such a thing—who would be greatest in the kingdom of God. Christ gave a very surprising response. What was it?

_____

_____

_____

Husbands and Wives

The next set of relationships Paul touches on is proper marriage relationships. These relationships should be built on the type of love and care Christ has for His bride, the church.

Ephesians 5:22, 24 and the last part of verse 33 deal with the attitudes women are to have toward their husbands. Paul probably put this first as women were questioning their new role based on being set free by Christ to serve God. But because the husband is given the authority as the head of the wife and family, I want to consider first what the godly husband's marching orders are. Then we will come back and look at the wife's tasks.

Roles for the Husband

2. From Ephesians 5:23 through the first part of verse 33, we have the view a spirit-filled, godly husband should demonstrate. List what you find.

_____

_____

_____

Again, it is important to emphasize, this is not possible without being filled with the Spirit. The husband is to display agape love, the kind of love that can only come from God Himself. Our ability to love with agape love comes from being filled with and controlled by the Spirit or Holy Ghost.

It is easy to love our wives if our wives are spirit-filled and submit to our leadership. But what if our wife is quite the opposite? The book of Hosea gives us an interesting look at a marriage relationship that mirrors God's love and pursuit of each one of us. Hosea is told to marry a prostitute who already has illegitimate children. After the marriage, the wife is rotten to the core, constantly chasing after her sinful lovers. God says in Hosea 2:6 that He will put a hedge of thorns around her so she cannot find her lovers. You see the hedge of thorns talked about in here is like the crown of thorns Christ wore at His crucifixion. They are normally from two to four inches long, extremely hard and tough, and razor sharp! They will rip anyone to shreds who tries to go through them. God in His mercy has put such a hedge around each of us. He knows we have fleshly lusts, but He jealously guards us from evil.

Note too, God does not merely forgive her sin. He has to expose it (Hosea 2:9-13). It must come out in the open so the wife has the chance to repent. Hard times and scars come when we wander into sin. Yet God says He will draw her back to Himself. When she does repent, God in essence says "Come here, my beloved. I want us to have an honest, holy relationship, where we are One. This relationship of betrothal will be based in righteousness, judgment, loving kindness, mercy, and faithfulness." (Hosea 2:14-20 paraphrased).

3. This very type of attitude is expressed in Ephesians 5:26-27. List what you find.

_____

_____

_____

4. God wants us to lead by example, by our sanctity. Look at John 17:17-19 and see what Christ had to say. Write down what you find.

_____

_____

_____

The truth of God's word is absolutely essential to ensuring your wife is and remains sanctified. Another aspect of the word of God is that it cleanses her by the washing of water by the word. This cleansing wash is the act of confession of our sins (1 John 1:9) and is vital to her personal growth.

5. Why is it so important to use the word of God according to Hebrews 4:12?

_____

_____

_____

We do not have the ability to look into our wife's heart and determine her motives for what she does. But I can fully trust the word of God to reveal it. As she learns to submit to God and His word, then she will continue to develop holiness or sanctity in her life.

Paul says the whole purpose of Christ toward His bride, the church, is to present her as a glorious, absolutely beautiful bride. She has outward beauty, but more importantly, she has inward beauty and purity of heart. Her wedding garment is not wrinkled or soiled. It too is spotless, being pure white through the cleansing power of the blood of the Lamb. Is that your desire for your wife, to have her walk with you as a holy, unblemished bride? Sometimes, we get lazy and reflect an attitude of, "It's her walk. Let her do as she sees fit." Christ always seeks the best, highest, and purest path for the walk of His bride.

In Ephesians 5:28-32, Paul talks about loving our wife the way we love our own body. It really is the second great commandment (see Leviticus 19:18). Well, guess who your closest neighbor is? Your closest neighbor was formed from your rib back in the Garden of Eden. The ribs protect all of the vital organs. So too is your closest neighbor, which is your wife. When you love her properly, you love yourself.

6. Look at the passage from Proverbs 31:10-12 and tell what you see.

_____

_____

_____

Roles for the Wife

7. Having briefly touched on the spirit-filled husbands' roles, now let's turn our attention to the spirit-filled wife as reflected in Ephesians 5:22-24, and the last part of verse 33. What roles do you see for the wife?

_____

_____

_____

8. One of the key items is that she is to submit to her husband as unto the Lord. In today's world, many women reject the attitude of submission and reverence of their husbands as arcane and irrelevant. Why?

_____

_____

_____

They base it on what they have seen in the relationships their parents demonstrated. Were their parents spirit-filled and submissive to each other? If you have not seen something work, it is hard to make it true in your own life.

9. Another reason is found back in Genesis. Look at the encounter between Eve and the serpent in Genesis 3:1-6. What was the serpent up to and what was its primary tactic?

_____

_____

_____

10. Now, compare what God had told Adam in Genesis 2 with Eve's words in Genesis 3. What differences did you find?

_____

_____

_____

11. Another key passage talks about a believing wife who faces a husband who does not obey the word of God. Look at 1 Peter 3:1-4 and put down what you find.

_____

_____

_____

Now let's look at reverence for her husband. The word for reverence means to fear exceedingly, to be frightened of, which then causes one to revere or respect them as one with authority and power. When a judge enters a courtroom, all the people rise as a symbol of respect to the position of judge. Note, I said the position, not the person. Some judges as people are contemptible, but the position is honorable, respectable, and held in high regard. This is the concept of reverence to the husband, recognizing his position as established by God as honorable and to be held in high regard.

Many women say this is an impossible task. Humanly speaking in the flesh, it really is. But if the wife is spirit-filled, she has a totally different mindset. She is looking to God's Holy Spirit to guide her, but also to guide and/or bring about change in her husband. When her husband is spirit-filled, then their relationship can grow and become what God wants for each and every married couple—a showcase for agape love in action.

Study 14: Building Strong Marriage Foundations (Part 2)
Ephesians 5:21-33

This study is based more on my personal observations in nearly four decades of marriage. Although not directly based on a specific verse in Ephesians 5:21-33, I felt these principles are worth sharing. They are written from the perspective of a husband, but I pray wives can learn from it also.

There are five basic foundational elements in any Godly marriage and family: common faith and zeal, sexual relations, communication, money, and raising children. We will touch briefly on the first four in this study. Raising children will be covered in a subsequent study.

Common Faith and Zeal

1. The first and foremost issue in a good marriage relationship is common faith and common zeal in Christ. The whole purpose of a Godly marriage must be based upon belief in Christ and both being filled with the Spirit. If the believers are not equal in their zeal for following God and Christ, problems can definitely arise. Look at Matthew 10:36-39 and 1 Kings 11:1-3 and put down what you see.

_____

_____

_____

You see, the wife has a special place of influence. She came from the rib of man. Now what do ribs protect? They protect vital organs of the body. So too, the woman should serve as a protection for her husband. As mentioned in a previous study, the enemy can trick her, just like he did in the Garden of Eden. The serpent tempted Eve by twisting the Word of God and enticing her through her fleshly wisdom and desires.

2. You should also have a common level of zeal for the Lord. I have observed many couples who were getting married. One was a strong follower of Christ and the other was lukewarm. What do you think the outcome of their union was? Did both become zealous to follow Christ? Look at Amos 3:3 and write what you see.

_____

_____

_____

Unfortunately, most of these marriages dissipate the stronger ones love for Christ. Should we dissolve such a marriage? Certainly not. God hates divorce. Look at 1 Peter 3:1-4.

1 Peter 3:1-4

"1   Likewise, ye wives, be in subjection to your own husbands; that, if any obey not the word, they also may without the word be won by the conversation of the wives;

2   While they behold your chaste conversation coupled with fear.

3   Whose adorning let it not be that outward adorning of plaiting the hair, and of wearing of gold, or of putting on of apparel;

4   But let it be the hidden man of the heart, in that which is not corruptible, even the ornament of a meek and quiet spirit, which is in the sight of God of great price." (KJV)

The woman is told to let her walk and attitude of the heart to shine brightly. Rather than nagging, her actions will speak much louder than words. Paul further highlights this in his first epistle to the Corinthians.

1 Corinthians 7:16 "For what knowest thou, O wife, whether thou shalt save thy husband? or how knowest thou, O man, whether thou shalt save thy wife?" (KJV)

Rather pray that God would intervene and draw your mate to Himself. This in turn will begin to establish the foundation for a God-honoring marriage.

To those who are thinking of getting married, they should ask the question, "Will this potential mate draw me closer to Christ or push me away from Christ?" If at all possible, your mate should be a helper who draws you closer to Christ, hence, you are walking in agreement. As Solomon found out, his heathen wives had a different agenda than following God. That is also why God describes the union of a man and a woman in Genesis 2:24 as the two become one flesh. They have a common faith, a common zeal to serve the Lord, and they grow stronger and closer together in unity. Pray that the Lord gives you both a common faith, zeal, and fullness of the Holy Ghost.

Sexual Relations

The sexual component is often described as the spark plug that drives the marriage vehicle. It is not the only part, but without the spark, the motor will not run and the car goes nowhere. Men and women view sex differently. The old saying, "Men are from Mars and women are from Venus," has a lot of merit. God made us different. Initially, most men are more interested in the quantity of sex, rather than its quality. We are ready for sexual climax very quickly, whereas the wife may take much longer.

3. Women crave romance. Men were good at it in courtship, but what happened to Romeo after the ceremony? If you give them little reminders of how special they are, your relationship can really blossom. What things would you suggest?

_____

_____

_____

From my experience, here are some simple ways to keep the courtship going: tell your spouse "I love you" daily, give your spouse sincere compliments and praises (meals, laundry, housekeeping, money management, yard work, car repairs, fixing the roof, etc.), keep giving little surprises to show your affection (unexpected little trinkets and flowers, a favorite meal, etc.), find time for just the two of you (in nearly 40 years of marriage, we have always had a date night every week), take time to find out which of your touches give your spouse sexual pleasure (try and find every one of them), and plan a special trip where the two of you can be alone (not interrupted by kids).

4. What other things would you add to the list?

_____

_____

_____

5. Another difficulty we have is learning how to communicate our sexual preferences. Sometimes men like to be the initiator, other times not. But how do you let your partner know your mood and vice versa?

_____

_____

_____

Each couple has to learn their own love language and how to interpret it. One way that may be helpful to initiate things is a simple list. First agree you both want to investigate ways to understand each other better sexually. Some people are really hung up on sex and do not want to talk about it. Sometimes bad experiences from the past make talking about sex very unpleasant.

6. Assuming you are both interested, then each of you take a piece of paper and write down two or three things you like most about your mate's lovemaking. Then write down two or three things you would like to see improved.

_____

_____

_____

Then make sure you have sufficient time to talk about it. You may need to take several different sessions to cover everything. And some things you will have to work on over a much longer time.

7. The key to great and lasting sexual pleasure is found in 1 Corinthians 7:3-5. What is it?

_____

_____

_____

When it comes to having sex with your spouse, note you do not have power over your body, but rather yield it to your spouse. What Paul is trying to communicate is your primary purpose in the sexual act is to please your mate and vice versa. When you both look at the sex act as an opportunity to first and foremost please your mate, then your time together will take on a totally different meaning and should become much more fulfilling.

Also note that Paul said sex was not to be used as a weapon. I am going to punish my mate by not having sex until I get my way. If we use sex as a reward or a means to get our way, then Paul indicates this type of behavior gives Satan an opportunity to tempt us into immoral behavior. Remember the objective of your sexual relationship is to meet the needs of your partner, even if it does not coincide with your own needs. Let your lovemaking be unselfish!

Communications

Communications between couples is every bit as vital as having sex. In fact, it covers a much wider area. Learning how to listen and show respect for each other is very important. Too often, I had to prove myself "right" in various matters under discussion. It shuts off communication. What is the point in trying to share my views if your way is always "right?" Or I would begrudgingly listen to very good suggestions, yet still do it my selfish way. Someone once said, "Listening is allowing others to change your thinking." Too often our minds are already made up. Don't confuse me with the facts! Our mates want to share their ideas, hopes, and desires for the relationship—to make it better. Learn to search out your mates ideas so each of you can contribute fully to building your relationship into oneness.

Often the biggest part of communication is finding the time and place to do it. In one home, we had a porch swing. We would sit and talk for a half hour or more, while we watched the kids play in our yard or in the neighbors' yard across the street. We tried to do this every day.

8. What are some ways you think would improve your communication with your mate?

_____

_____

_____

On the next page are some simple rules that have helped guide us in building a good communications foundation. They are useful in establishing good communications in any relationship, whether it be husband and wife, parents and children, employer and employee, or next door neighbors.

Rules for Effective Communication

Invariably, in every marriage relationship disagreements will arise. How you resolve these "issues" will greatly determine the growth and success of your marriage. You will either grow closer together and to Christ or you will grow further apart from each other and Christ. I pray these simple guidelines will help you in communicating with your spouse.

+ <u>Never in anger</u> (count to twenty before you speak).

+ <u>Don't let the sun go down on your anger</u> (Try to start the resolution process within 24 hours. Actual resolution may take days.).

+ <u>Set aside enough time</u> (trying to fix things when you have to leave for work in three minutes usually causes more problems).

+ <u>Set aside a place</u> (privacy is important as little eyes and ears pick up a lot, both positive and negative).

+ <u>Pray for Godly love and understanding</u> (versus an attitude that I am the boss and we will do it my way!).

+ <u>No character assassinations</u> (Examples: You're never were honest. You are a real slob. How could I have ever married an idiot like you?).

+ <u>Talk quietly to each other</u> (whenever the decibel level during the conversation goes up, communication goes down).

+ <u>Listen, then try and verbalize what you think the other person said</u> (our imagination can run wild and add a lot of implied slights that were never intended).

+ <u>Be honest without being brutal</u> (remember how Christ deals with your sins—with mercy, grace, and compassion).

+ <u>When you are wrong, admit it</u> (versus my pride which keeps me from admitting I am wrong).

+ <u>Tears are a time for tenderness and comfort.</u>

+ <u>Once settled—forgive, forget, and move on.</u>

Money Management

9. Money causes as many arguments and disputes as anything in many marriages. Marriages today have elaborate pre-nuptial agreements to protect money and other assets in the event divorce occurs. So what will help your marriage have a solid financial foundation? Three things come to mind—budgeting, saving, and limiting credit card use. What other things would you add?

_____

_____

_____

Too many people never budget their money. They spend compulsively. That is why all of those neat little items are stacked at the checkout counters. Buy an extra candy bar, a comb, a magazine, etc. Whenever my wife shops for groceries, she always has a list based on the meals she has planned for the week. She will spend maybe $120. But if I do the shopping with the same list, the bill comes out $235. Why? Because I see things I want, not what our meals require. The same applies to clothing purchases and other reoccurring purchases. Today, many of us fall into the fast food habit. Who has time to cook anymore? A fast food meal for two (depending on where you eat) costs from $12-$25. A well planned meal at home is frequently less than $7. All of that adds up over the course of a month. Try keeping track of every cent you spend for one month. Then analyze it and see how much you could save with some discipline and a simple action plan.

By developing a budget, you can determine how much money you can afford to spend on various items. A rule of thumb is about 30% of your after taxes income should be used against rent or a home mortgage. Another 15% can be allocated against a vehicle. The remaining 50% must cover everything else—food, clothing, medical expenses and insurance, school materials, utility bills, car maintenance, retirement savings, life insurance, tithing at church, etc. When I did an analysis of my expenses, I came up with my monthly income needs of $4,000. However, the income my wife and I brought in only amounted to $3,500. I either have to get another job or cut expenses. The budgeting process helps me to plan and make adjustments.

Also, find out who is the better money manager—you or your spouse? Let whoever does it best run the checking accounts, pay bills, etc.

You may also want to set guidelines for the use of credit cards. What items will you use it for—gasoline, groceries, vacations, a home theater entertainment center, etc.? A good rule of thumb is only using your credit card up to the amount you can pay off every month. If your budget allocates $500 towards credit card debt, then pay that amount every month. Think of how much you will save by not paying any interest charges. If you find you are spending a lot more than you should, cut up the cards!

Study 15: Raising Children

Ephesians 6:1-4

Ephesians 6:1-4

"1 Children, obey your parents in the Lord: for this is right.

2 Honour thy father and mother; (which is the first commandment with promise;)

3 That it may be well with thee, and thou mayest live long on the earth.

4 And, ye fathers, provoke not your children to wrath: but bring them up in the nurture and admonition of the Lord." (KJV)

This study continues the results of being Spirit-filled with respect to relationships of parents and particularly fathers with our children. Both parents are involved in directing and requiring obedience from their children. The children are to honor and respect their parents. However, Paul makes an interesting statement in Ephesians 6:4. He says "fathers" not "parents". Consequently, in the first part of this study, we will examine the interaction of fathers with their children.

The Unique Position of the Father

1. Before we address what Paul says to the children, let us first look at what he says in Ephesians 6:4. Write down who Paul is talking to and what he says.

_____

_____

_____

Notice who has the responsibility for not provoking your children to wrath and bringing them up in the nurture and admonition of the Lord—it is the father, not the mother, and not both parents. Authority for rules and right living must emanate from the father. Once the parents discuss what rules they will make, then the father is the one who must pronounce them to the children. Both parents must enforce the rules, but discipline for infractions rests with the father. Let's take a look at how this might work.

Let's assume the father with the mother's agreement has made a simple rule—come straight home from school and no playing at friend's houses until homework is done. Both parents call the child into the room and the father explains the rule.

2. The father then asks the child if there are any questions. If there are none, a good technique is to ask the child to repeat the rule. Why?

_____

_____

_____

So the rule is understood by both parents and the child. The child asks to go over to a friend's house. The mother says, "No, not until you finish your homework." The child doesn't want to do the homework, so the child finds the father and asks the same question (without revealing what the mother had said). The father says, "Sure, be home for supper." When the child comes home and is confronted by the mother, the child says, "Daddy said I could go."

3. There are several points at play here. What do you see?

_____

_____

_____

Had the father remembered the rule about homework, then he would not have given his permission. Children get confused by such inconsistencies. They even try and exploit them, playing one parent off against the other. Parents need to check with each other to avoid similar loopholes.

4. But let's say the father got it right and said, "Is your homework complete?" The child said, "Yes it is." So Dad says, "Be home for supper." In this case, the child lied and knowingly broke the rule. What comes next is extremely important—the fair and consistent enforcement of appropriate discipline. If one parent blows it off, "Give the kid a break this time. It is such a beautiful day anyway," then what does this teach the child?

_____

_____

_____

5. As you look back over these examples, how would you have handled it? Would you have even made such a rule? Was the rule fair?

_____

_____

_____

6. Now, let's get back to the second part of Ephesians 6:4 where it talks about not provoking your children to wrath. What are some instances in your life where your parents got you really mad or treated you unfairly?

_____

_____

_____

How can we provoke our children to wrath? What is Paul talking about? Because fathers set the rules of the household, they can be too strict and overly critical of their kids. It can crush their spirit, initiative, and spontaneity. They become discouraged, resentful, and bitter over time. Also, another way to cause wrath and bitterness in our children is when we show favoritism. We give one child different treatment than the other children. This can have serious repercussions.

7. Look at what happened to Joseph because of his father Jacob's favoritism toward him over his older brothers in Genesis 37:3-4, 18, 23-28. Put down what you see.

_____

_____

_____

8. Now, let's return to the last part of Ephesians 6:4. What does it mean to bring them up in the nurture and admonition of the Lord?

_____

_____

_____

The word for nurture implies to cause to grow through training and education, which also includes chastening or correcting. It is the whole learning process. We teach our children what is right based on the Word of God such as the Ten Commandments.

9. Look at God's formula for this in Deuteronomy 6:4-7. Put down what you find.

_____

_____

_____

This passage also infers that in every facet of our lives, we are to teach our children the principles that are true in our own walk with Christ. If something is not true in our life, then we cannot really teach it to our kids.

10. Another idea about nurture and admonition comes from the relationship of a nurse or care-giver babysitting children placed in her care. Look at 1 Thessalonians 2:7-8 and list the things you find.

_____

_____

_____

The care-giver cherishes the children, protects them, and is even willing to protect them with her life. A story I heard once illustrates this principle. In the days of steam locomotives, they would cast off lots of sparks as they went along the train tracks. This frequently caused fires in the plains states like Nebraska and Kansas where wheat and corn were cash crops. One farmer saw a fire coming toward his home started by a spark from a passing train. In order to save his house, he had to set his cornfields on fire. He hoped this would form a fire break, causing the fire to go around his home. In fact, it worked. As he was looking around the cornfields he had burned, he noticed a dead chicken lying on the ground. He kicked the dead carcass over and guess what he found? There were six baby chickens alive underneath their mother. She gave her life for her babies, which is what our attitude as fathers ought to be as we bring up our children in God's nurture and admonition.

11. Another good example of nurture and admonition comes from looking at and comparing the roles of two very different types of shepherds found in Ezekiel and the Psalms.

    a.   Put down what you see in Ezekiel 34:2-4.

_____

_____

_____

    b.   Now put down what you see in Psalms 23:1-6.

_____

_____

_____

The first shepherd is the hireling. He doesn't really care about the sheep (or I like to substitute children for sheep), except for what he can get for himself. He doesn't ensure they are properly fed or take them to the doctor when they are sick. By contrast, look at the good shepherd. His sheep or children do not want. He makes them do what is best for them, giving them a secure and peaceful home. He leads by example and helps the child choose Christ. Even when times are tough, the shepherd is always there, undergirding the child. They have imparted faith to them so they know who to place their real trust in—Jesus Christ.

Fathers, I pray you raise your children in such a way that they and your whole family will be viewed by God as He viewed Abraham and his household.

Genesis 18:19
"19 For I know him, that he will command his children and his household after him, and they shall keep the way of the LORD, to do justice and judgment; that the LORD may bring upon Abraham that which he hath spoken of him." (KJV)

Instructions to Children

Having laid the foundation for parents and fathers toward the children, what does Ephesians say to the children?

12. God lays it out very simply. Children obey your parents in the Lord as it is the right thing to do. Honor your parents. Treat them with respect. Listen to them and do what they instruct you to do. Why?

_____

_____

_____

Parents need to set rules, limits or boundaries for proper conduct for their children. Children want such boundaries, but they also want to see how far they can push the limits or go beyond them before the parent reacts. Each child must realize when they disobey their parents they should expect consistent and fair correction and admonishment. Sometimes they may make a mistake because the situation has never come up before. But when they know the rule and deliberately disobey it, then the parents must discipline them. Discipline can take many forms. Several passages in Proverbs talk about disciplining children through the use of a rod, which is a reference to spanking.

Proverbs 22:15
"15 Foolishness is bound in the heart of a child; but the rod of correction shall drive it far from him." (KJV)

Proverbs 23:13-14
"13 Withhold not correction from the child: for if thou beatest him with the rod, he shall not die.
14 Thou shalt beat him with the rod, and shalt deliver his soul from hell." (KJV)

Proverbs 29:15
"15 The rod and reproof give wisdom: but a child left to himself bringeth his mother to shame." (KJV)

13. This idea of spanking is hotly debated in our society today. What is your opinion about it?

_____

_____

_____

Many would call this child abuse, but it is God's way. Now it can become abusive, especially if it is done in anger. Remember one critical rule when giving our discipline—**never in anger**. When you choose to discipline your children, whether through spanking or verbally, you must be in control of your emotions. Otherwise, children may wind up with broken bones or psychological scars from yelling outbursts like, "You are an idiot. You never do anything right. Get out of my sight, you moron."

14. But if you choose spanking as a method of administering discipline to the seat of learning, how much is enough?

_____

_____

_____

15. Sometimes the rod will not give you enough leverage with very stubborn children. What do you do then?

_____

_____

_____

16. Ultimately, the parent should want what God wants for His children. Look at Hebrews 12:7-11 and list what you find.

_____

_____

_____

May each of us always bring up our children in a way pleasing to the Lord—with love, leadership and consistent admonition and nurturing.

Study 16: Employee-Employer Relationships
Ephesians 6:5-9

Ephesians 6:5-9

"5 Servants, be obedient to them that are your masters according to the flesh, with fear and trembling, in singleness of your heart, as unto Christ;

6 Not with eyeservice, as menpleasers; but as the servants of Christ, doing the will of God from the heart;

7 With good will doing service, as to the Lord, and not to men:

8 Knowing that whatsoever good thing any man doeth, the same shall he receive of the Lord, whether he be bond or free.

9 And, ye masters, do the same things unto them, forbearing threatening: knowing that your Master also is in heaven; neither is there respect of persons with him." (KJV)

This study looks at what God says to servants and masters, which in today's terms are employees and employers. You must remember in Paul's day, servants were considered property with no rights or freedom. If the master wanted a servant killed, even without a cause, the master was not breaking any law. He had absolute right to do whatever he wanted to with his property.

Many of the early believers were servants or slaves. Yet Christ had set everyone free. Consequently, those who were servants started to rebel against their masters. After all, they had been set free by the King of Kings.

The Roles for Servants or Employees

1. Paul shows us how God views such relationships. As an employee, look at verse 5 and put down key attitudes you see.

_____

_____

_____

One key is listening to what our employer says. Do we intently and very carefully listen to what he or she says? Perhaps you remember an old commercial about the investment firm of E.F. Hutton. It showed an investment broker for E.F. Hutton sitting in a restaurant with a client. When the broker spoke, suddenly everyone else in the restaurant leaned over so they could listen in on what was being said. The punch line was "When E.F. Hutton talks, people listen." This is the kind of attitude we are to display to our employer. When the employer speaks, we should stop what we are doing and give them our full attention.

2. Another key point mentioned in verse 5 is acting in singleness of heart as unto the Lord. Why is this important? Look at Matthew 6:24 and see what you can discover.

_____

_____

_____

What Paul is trying to get us to understand is that we are to serve our bosses with the same kind of devotion and loyalty as we do in our service to God. Paul goes on to describe it as giving our service in our workplace as an offering to God. We are trying to please God with our diligence, not just trying to please a human boss.

Have you ever been around someone who constantly goofs off when the boss is not around? However, as soon as the boss shows up, they act like they are the busiest worker there. They are men pleasers, who only work when under direct observation. That is not the attitude of a believer as we are truly serving our one Master, Jesus Christ.

The Roles for Masters or Employers

3. Ephesians 6:9 gives a very simple set of instructions to those of us who are employers. Write down what you see.

_____

_____

_____

4. Employers have the same type of attitude that you expect from your employees—respect and do not threaten or brow-beat them. Look at Colossians 4:1. What else does it say to employers?

_____

_____

_____

Give your employees what is just. Think of just this way—Christ is standing next to you when you tell employees what their pay and benefits will be. Will Christ approve? Then you should give equal pay for equal work. This injustice was just corrected by a law signed by President Obama that requires equal pay between men and women when their jobs are essentially the same.

You should also care for them just like they are part of your family. Are we willing to build them up and encourage them or do we like to run roughshod over them? A boss is in a unique position to wield power over others. Rather than treat them like property, they should care for them and treat them with respect. Employers have the same ultimate boss as an employee—God! And God does not show any respect because of your earthly position.

5. Look at Matthew 24:45-51. What attributes do you see?

    a.   The wise servant or employer

_____

_____

_____

    b.   The evil servant or horrible employer

_____

_____

_____

    c.   What is the end result for both of them?

_____

_____

_____

6. James 5:1-4 has equally strong words to the rich. Put down what you find.

_____

_____

_____

Whether we are employees or employers, we have only one Master, Jesus Christ. He will reward us based on how diligent and productive we are and how we treat those working with or for us.

Study 17: Finally, Stand against the Wiles of the Devil!

Ephesians 6:10-12

Ephesians 6:10-12

"10 Finally, my brethren, be strong in the Lord, and in the power of his might.

11 Put on the whole armour of God, that ye may be able to stand against the wiles of the devil.

12 For we wrestle not against flesh and blood, but against principalities, against powers, against the rulers of the darkness of this world, against spiritual wickedness in high places." (KJV)

These last few verses in this final chapter of Ephesians conclude the process of growing to maturity in Christ—going from sitting, to walking and finally to standing. Paul begins by addressing the believers, not as dear children as in chapter five, but rather as my brethren. When you get to this point in your walk with Christ, you are no longer children but maturing adults.

1. Paul is quick to remind us about the key to being able to stand. What is it?

_____

_____

_____

2. Another passage, John 15:5 (you may want to read it in context from verses 1-5), gives us additional insights. What are they?

_____

_____

_____

3. Paul gives us another view of this battleground in 2 Corinthians 10:4-5. Paul tells us how to combat these various attacks of the enemy. Write the things you see.

_____

_____

_____

The Origin of Strongholds

A Thought→An Action→A Habit→A Character→A Destiny

Strongholds all begin with just a thought. The thought causes you to take an action. If you keep repeating the action, it becomes a habit or stronghold. As you allow the stronghold to remain, it becomes your character. And your character determines your eternal destiny.

4. Let's see how this might work. You see a beautiful woman walking down the street. Is that a sin? No, the first instinctive look is not a sin. It is a God-given reflex related to self-preservation. But what happens if we allow the image to dwell in our mind? You decide or choose to take a second and much longer look at her. From a sexual perspective, you may begin to fantasize having sex with her. Is that a sin? Jesus described it in Matthew 5:28. What did He say?

_____

_____

_____

The simple action of taking a second look turns into sin. If the act of taking a second look is not dealt with properly, then it can become a habit or stronghold in your life. In the case of sexual lust, this often leads men to pornography, which can easily become a destructive addiction. As you allow the enemy to fortify this stronghold, casual attempts to evict him are easily rebuffed. We begin to lose our desire for spiritual things, which can lead us to a character of fruitlessness for God. Its destiny can be catastrophic.

5. Let's look at this now from a woman's perspective. You are working in the yard before you husband gets home from work. You notice your next door neighbor is putting in some shrubs. He is very attractive. As you stop and chat, he offers you a beer and invites you into his house. Has sin entered into the equation yet? How would you respond?

_____

_____

_____

6. Are there other seemingly innocent interactions that have led to problems in your life?

_____

_____

_____

7. Read Galatians 5:19-21 and see which areas may be strongholds or battlegrounds in your life. Ask the Holy Spirit to help you in examining this passage so you give honest answers.

_____

_____

_____

Did you catch the last part of Galatians 5:21? They which do such things, those who habitually practice strongholds, are deceiving themselves. If they think they will inherit the kingdom of God, they may be sadly mistaken. Another pertinent passage talks about what we sow or allow to enter our minds and lives.

Galatians 6:7-8

"7 Be not deceived; God is not mocked: for whatsoever a man soweth, that shall he also reap.

8   For he that soweth to his flesh shall of the flesh reap corruption; but he that soweth to the Spirit shall of the Spirit reap life everlasting." (KJV)

8. Sometimes evil thoughts come in when you are right in the middle of praying. Where do you think these thoughts come from? Satan is the source, shooting one of his fiery darts at you. So what do you do to overcome these thoughts?

_____

_____

_____

First, you must realize you do have a choice. You can dwell on the thought, examine it, ask questions about it, take action on it, or you can reject it. You do not have to let the thought make a pit stop in your head. Reject it when you recognize its source or intention. In the name of Christ and by His blood, command it to get out! We are to make no provision for the flesh. There should be an immediate "No Vacancy" sign to point to. Pray a simple prayer like this:

"In the name of Jesus Christ, I reject these thoughts. I claim His blood to cleanse me. Create in me a clean heart and mind. Set a watch over my eyes that I may see things with the pure eyes of Christ. I ask this in Jesus name. Amen."

The Sin of Pride

When we reach a pinnacle in our walk with Christ and are standing as warriors, one temptation or wile usually shows up. It's called PRIDE.

9. The enemy whispers, "You are such a strong and mature Christian. You finally have earned God's respect and are a real warrior." What is the problem here?

_____

_____

_____

By feeling you have earned God's respect, it means you are now standing based on your merit, on what you have accomplished. Pride puffs us up and soon we are ready for a hard fall. When you look at the word PRIDE, it frequently reflects a pyramid:

I

SIN

PRIDE

LUCIFER

Ultimately, "I" is at the center of the pyramid—I have done it and deserve proper respect for my accomplishments. This is one of the first temptations or wiles of the devil you will encounter when you stand as a warrior.

The issue is one of power—self versus God, is one of the most important battle grounds. How do you win this battle? A lot of it depends on us gaining a true view of ourselves—seeing ourselves as God sees us. Just look at the church at Laodicea. They thought they had need of nothing!

Revelation 3:17-18

"17 Because thou sayest, I am rich, and increased with goods, and have need of nothing; and knowest not that thou art wretched, and miserable, and poor, and blind, and naked:

18 I counsel thee to buy of me gold tried in the fire, that thou mayest be rich; and white raiment, that thou mayest be clothed, and that the shame of thy nakedness do not appear; and anoint thine eyes with eyesalve, that thou mayest see." (KJV)

They were way off the mark. We need the same type of vision to see ourselves as God sees us. Let's look briefly at the example of three men of God: Isaiah, Daniel, and Job. Look at the following passages and see what you can find.

10. Isaiah 6:1-5

_____

_____

_____

11. Daniel 10:7-8

_____

_____

_____

12. Job 42:5-6

_____

_____

_____

Casting Down Imaginations

Now let's turn our attention back to 2 Corinthians 10:5. The first object of our warfare is the casting down of imaginations. Imaginations are thoughts coming out of the heart.

1 Chronicles 28:9

"9   And thou, Solomon my son, know thou the God of thy father, and serve him with a perfect heart and with a willing mind: for the LORD searcheth all hearts, and understandeth all the imaginations of the thoughts: if thou seek him, he will be found of thee; but if thou forsake him, he will cast thee off for ever." (KJV)

13. People think they have all the wisdom and they can ignore what God says. Look at what transpired with Adam, Eve, and the serpent. Read over Genesis 2:16 through 3:7. What errors did you see?

_____

_____

_____

14. In this dialogue between Eve and the Serpent, what was the primary tactic the enemy used?

_____

_____

_____

He attacked the word of God. "Yea, hath God said?" He wants us to doubt God's Word. He appealed to her vanity by inferring God was giving her a bum deal. God did not want her to know everything like God did. You can be just like God. Finally, after listening to his arguments, she took a look. She rationalized it is a good food source, it is beautiful to look at, and besides, it is a good thing to want to be wise. So she convinced herself to give it a try. Then she offered it to Adam. He still had time to save himself by refusing it. But he allowed his wife to lead him into the arms of sin.

Today, many feel there is no absolute right and wrong. Gay priests and marriages are okay. They say there is no such thing as guilt, "I'm OK, and you're OK." But God is not mocked and His word stands true forever.

Casting Down High Things Opposed to the Knowledge of God.

Please note it says high things opposed to the knowledge of God. High things, things of reputation, things the world tells us to emulate, things that make us proud, advanced things, and the like are snares to draw us in the wrong direction. If we were doing blatantly wrong things, people would react with, "They are getting what they deserve."

15. But the high and powerful things of this world oppose the knowledge of God. Romans 1:18-32 speaks to this. Put down what you find.

_____

_____

_____

16. Another high thing is abortion. A woman has the right to choose. Yet listen to what the Psalmist says in Psalm 139:13-16. Pay particular attention to verse 16. Write what you see.

_____

_____

_____

Greed and corruption are other forms of high things opposed to the knowledge of God. The Enron case is a perfect example of greed and corruption. The ordinary worker lost everything as most of their savings program consisted of Enron stock. Yet, the high level executives left with millions of dollars. Another Chief Executive Officer was given a multi-million dollar bonus when the ordinary workers in the company were forced to take pay cuts in order to avoid bankruptcy. There are several passages you need to examine.

17. Listen to what James 5:1-7 says and write what you see.

_____

_____

_____

18. Look at 1 Timothy 6:9-12 and put down what you find.

_____

_____

_____

19. Finally, look at Matthew 13:22 and see what it says.

_____

_____

_____

20. One final high thing we want to examine briefly is counterfeits. We see counterfeiting in worship. People know how to say the right words, but their actions reflect a form of godliness and are divest of His power. Look at these two passages, Matthew 7:21-23 and 2 Timothy 3:1-5 and put what you find.

_____

_____

_____

Bring Every Thought Captive

21. The final admonition concerns our thought life. We are to bring every thought captive to the obedience of Christ. How do you think this happens?

_____

_____

_____

This idea of bringing every thought into captivity to the obedience of Christ is the strategic start of using the whole armour of God. Remember, what it says you must do **before** you put on the whole armour of God? Be strong in the Lord and the power of His might! You see, if we think it is your job to bring every thought into captivity, if you think you must use the armour of God yourself, then you will soon find you have failed miserably. The "I" cannot bring every thought captive. Our fleshly thoughts and lusts do not want to bring every thought captive to obeying Christ. It takes the power of His might to make the armour effective.

Let's look at an illustration using a work glove. What can it do by itself? It can do nothing. But when you put your hand into the glove, what happens? It takes on the character of your hand and can do whatever you hand can do. It is the same way we must use the armour of God to bring every thought captive to the obedience of Christ.

Keep Your Eyes on the Master

Remember, the goal of using the whole armour of God is to be able to withstand in the evil day, and having done all, to stand. A key passage to help you in your warfare is found in Hebrews 12:1-2. Sin easily entangles us. Have you ever tried to run a race with both legs in a burlap sack? It is really hard to go very fast. We keep getting tripped up. The same thing happens in a three legged race, where you tie one leg to someone else. Sin easily trips us up. It weighs us down. Guilt, depression, and despair crush our spirits. But what does the passage tell us to do? Lay it aside. Strip off the dead weight. Confess and forsake the sin and do not look back and have a pity party. Instead, get your focus and your faith on Jesus. He started the work of faith in you and He will finish it. You cannot change your past, so stop worrying about it and looking over your shoulder. Christ has already dealt with the condemnation and penalties associated with your past and nailed them to the Cross. Give Him thanks for that provision and press forward, keeping your eyes on the Master daily.

Study 18: Wiles of the Devil against the Churches (Part 1)
Revelation 2:1 - 29

The next two studies look at the subtle and deceptive tactics the devil uses on the churches. The enemy works hardest inside the churches. We will start in Revelation, chapter two.

The Church at Ephesus (Revelation 2:1-7)

1. Ephesus looks like a pretty strong church. List the good things they do.

_____

_____

_____

2. They have a very impressive list of accomplishments and attitudes. So what is the problem?

_____

_____

_____

The Church at Smyrna (Revelation 2:8-11)

3. Here the church is under tribulation. Its ranks have been infiltrated by those who say they are believers, but they really are in the enemy's camp. False believers may sound good at first, but try the spirit within them. Also what are some of the other weapons the enemy uses on this church?

_____

_____

_____

Fear is always a big tip off that the enemy is actively attacking. When the enemy reminds us that sufferings will be attached to it, our fear can get even stronger. And there is one more subtle trick—"Quit!" God only allows tribulation to last for a set period of time. Ten days, ten years—the enemy wants you to look at your circumstances rather than the One who is in charge. Remember what happened to Job. All his wealth, children, servants, and health were stripped away. His wife told him to curse God and die. His friends tried counseling him in order for him to discover what his errors were. Yet, Job remained true to what he felt in his heart. Surely, do you really think God is in charge? Again, the enemy attacks the truthfulness and character of God.

The Church at Pergamos (Revelation 2:12-17)

Satan has become entrenched in this church. Compromise and accommodation are everywhere. Rather than rebuffing that which is evil, they are now content to dwell with the enemy.

4. This goes against the whole counsel of the first Psalm. Look at Psalms1:1-2 and put what down what you see.

_____

_____

_____

5. So what was their real problem according to this Psalm?

_____

_____

_____

In the church at Pergamos, they even allowed false teachings to occur. They also did not hate what God hates—the Nicolaitans' doctrine. While no specific passage describes what that doctrine was, a clue comes from the name in Greek. It refers to the division of clergy from lay people—a division. Rather than an equal brotherhood, now clergy were given authority over laity.

The Church at Thyatira (Revelation 2:18-29)

This church did many good works, displaying love, service, faith and patience. In fact, Christ commended them for their staying power. Their latter efforts were even more productive than what happened at the start of this church.

6. But Christ has some things against this church. What are they?

_____

_____

_____

7. To those believers who did not partake of these doctrines and wicked actions, Christ gave one final instruction. What was it and what do you think it means?

_____

_____

_____

Study 19: Wiles of the Devil against the Churches (Part 2)
Revelation 3:1 - 19

In the letters to the churches in Revelation chapter two, we see a lot of good works being done. But a lot of subtle missing of the mark occurs. The work of the church becomes more important than our love for Christ. Believers were not checking out what people were teaching, searching the Word to see if those things were so. Consequently, false teachings and sexual fornication sprung up in the churches. Fear of suffering and the urge to quit were also present. These are ways the enemy works today in the churches. Now let us continue into Revelation chapter three.

The Church at Sardis (Revelation 3:1-6)

1. Those in this church have all the right language—born again, repentance, redeemed by the blood, yet God says they are DEAD! What do you think was the problem?

_____

_____

_____

2. What does Jeremiah 17:9 says about our heart? Is it applicable to this church?

_____

_____

_____

3. James 2:14-17 has another symptom present in this church. What is it?

_____

_____

_____

4. Another area mentioned is their garments are defiled by sin. Look at Jude 23 and put down the key attitude you see.

_____

_____

_____

Again, there was no stand against wickedness in the church. Please note the severe warning Christ gives in Revelation 3:5. He can blot our names out of the Lambs Book of Life. Re-examine to see if you are practicing what God has revealed to you from His word. If you need change, repent and turn back to God and do it His way. Stay alert and watch for the return of Christ!

The Church at Philadelphia (Revelation 3:7-13)

5. They were given an open door by God, which no man can shut. They were faithful in keeping or obeying the word and not denying they were followers of Christ. However, there is a reference to their having but a little strength. What do you think might cause such a remark? Look at 2 Corinthians 4:6-9 and John 15:1-5 for possible clues.

_____

_____

_____

6. Note too the chilling admonition in Revelation 3:11, "Let no man take thy crown." What does that mean? Look at John 10:10 and Malachi 3:10-12 and see what you can discover.

_____

_____

_____

7. Two passages, 2 Peter 1:4 and Hebrews 11:6, may give you some added insights. Write what you find.

_____

_____

_____

The Church at Laodicea (Revelation 3:15-19)

8. This church had a very high opinion of their standing before God. List the things they said about themselves.

_____

_____

_____

9. But our opinion and view of ourselves is frequently very different than God's view of us. How did God see this church?

_____

_____

_____

10. Revelation 3:18 gives a list of things God said they needed to pursue. Tell me how you think you can make those things true in your life.

_____

_____

_____

The concluding words to the church at Laodicea are important: "As many as I love, I rebuke and chasten: be zealous therefore, and repent." God is a jealous God and because of His love for us, He will not let us be deceived by the enemy. Welcome His chastening and be willing to forsake whatever sinful desires, thoughts, or actions He reveals. I must depend on God to enlighten me and keep me on the narrow pathway. I cannot trust my own instincts and heart.

Jeremiah 17:9-10
"9 The heart is deceitful above all things, and desperately wicked: who can know it?
10 I the LORD search the heart, I try the reins, even to give every man according to his ways, and according to the fruit of his doings." (KJV)

The Psalmist points us to the only solution that will work—allow God to do the searching and allow God to show and lead you in the way you should go.

Psalms 139:23-24
"23 Search me, O God, and know my heart: try me, and know my thoughts:
24 And see if there be any wicked way in me, and lead me in the way everlasting." (KJV)

The church at Laodicea thought they had it all. They had need of nothing, or so they thought. How many are rocking along in church thinking this is really what following God is all about? Is this the power of God at work? No, that is why so many feel the church is irrelevant today. We have great churches and programs, but very little demonstration of the Spirit and His power.

1 Corinthians 2:4-5 (KJV)
"4 And my speech and my preaching was not with enticing words of man's wisdom, but in demonstration of the Spirit and of power:
5 That your faith should not stand in the wisdom of men, but in the power of God."

If we are to stay strong in the power of His might and be able to put on and use the full armor of God, we must depend on Him to show us our wicked ways. Then we must repent and turn to the path He directs.

Well, there are many other tricks the enemy will try and pull on you. On the next page are some other passages you may want to look at.

For Further Study—Other Wiles of the Devil

Things of the world: 1 John 2:15-16

Lack of knowledge: Hosea 4:6, Matthew 13:18-19

Riches: Matthew 13:22; 1 Timothy 6:10

Deceit: Mark 13:22; Ephesians 4:14

Unforgiveness: 2 Corinthians 2:10-11

Mind Games: blinded 2 Corinthians 4:4; too simple 2 Corinthians 11:3

False Teachers: 2 Corinthians 11:13-15; 2 Thessalonians 2:9-12

Love unrighteousness: 2 Thessalonians 2:9-12

Tolerance of sin: Revelation 2:20; 1 Corinthians 5:1-2

No fear of the Lord: Proverbs 8:13

Absence of Faith: 1 Chronicles 21:1; Matthew 7:21-23

Carnal or Immature: 1 Corinthians 3:1-3

Study 20: Take and Put on the Whole Armour of GOD and Stand!

Ephesians 6:13-18

Ephesians 6:13-18

"13 Wherefore take unto you the whole armour of God, that ye may be able to withstand in the evil day, and having done all, to stand.

14 Stand therefore, having your loins girt about with truth, and having on the breastplate of righteousness;

15 And your feet shod with the preparation of the gospel of peace;

16 Above all, taking the shield of faith, wherewith ye shall be able to quench all the fiery darts of the wicked.

17 And take the helmet of salvation, and the sword of the Spirit, which is the word of God:

18 Praying always with all prayer and supplication in the Spirit, and watching thereunto with all perseverance and supplication for all saints;" (KJV)

This is the final study on Ephesians. Paul tells us to take and put on the whole armour of God for two principle purposes: withstanding the assaults of Satan in the evil day and at the end of our time on this earth to be standing for God. I can remember as a young child, we used to play "King of the Mountain." We would wrestle each other and see who the last one on top of the hill was. That is a picture of what God wants for each of His children—to be standing strong in their faith in Christ until they are called home.

Please note two things before we start looking at each individual component of the armour. First we must use <u>all</u> of the components of the armour. If you omit one or two components, then you are very vulnerable to attack. Secondly, whose armour is it? It is God's armour and not yours. Now let us examine the components of the armour of God.

Loins Girt about with Truth

1. The first one is, "Stand therefore, having your loins girt about with truth." It is very interesting that the armour starts with the loins—the place of our sexual desires. We are instructed to gird our loins with truth. Psalms 119:9-11 tells us one way to make this happen in our life. Write what you see in that passage.

_____

_____

_____

Another study about girding your loins with truth comes out of the book of Proverbs. The first three chapters are words of wisdom from a father to his son. I encourage you to look at these chapters and go over them very slowly. Ask God to open up your understanding in order that you may hear and do them.

2. Another reason we gird our loins with truth comes from Hebrews 4:12-16. Put down what you find.

_____

_____

_____

The Breastplate of Righteousness

The next component of the armour of God is, "Stand therefore . . . having on the breastplate of righteousness." The breastplate is a very visible part of the armour and it protects a lot of vital organs—the heart, the lungs, liver, etc.

3. But what is the breastplate of righteousness? Several passages give us insight: Jeremiah 23:6, 1 Corinthians 1:30-31, Philippians 3:8-9, 1 Thessalonians 5:8 and Matthew 6:33. From these passages, how would you describe the breastplate of righteousness?

_____

_____

_____

You see the LORD is our breastplate. He is our righteousness. Its characteristic is faith and love, which is activated as we seek Him first. Listen to what David said when he faced Goliath.

1 Samuel 17:47
"47 And all this assembly shall know that the LORD saveth not with sword and spear: for the battle is the LORD's, and he will give you into our hands." (KJV)

It always comes back to where is your focus and faith—in your strength or in His? When the enemy sees Christ is your breastplate, he must look for other areas to attack you.

Gospel Footprints

The next one mentioned concerns your feet. "Stand therefore, having . . . your feet shod with the preparation of the gospel of peace." There are three aspects of this I want you to consider.

The use of the word preparation of the gospel of peace refers to an ointment or perfume on your feet. If you have ever had the unpleasant experience of someone taking their shoes off followed by a foul smell, then you get the idea of how the odor can turn people off. If our steps and footprints give off a sweet aroma, then it is not offensive.

Another word for odor is "savour", which can mean taste or aroma. When Mom cooks a pie, it has a sweet taste and puts off a wonderful smell. When you walk in the kitchen, you know something really good is there.

4. Look at 2 Corinthians 2:14-16 and write what you find.

_____

_____

_____

5. The second aspect of your footprint is fairly simple. Why do you need your feet shod or why do you need to wear shoes?

_____

_____

_____

The third aspect of your footprint is reflected in a promise in Genesis 3:15. It talks about the seed of women bruising the serpents' head. But what happens to the one who steps on the snakes head? Their heel gets bruised. We are in spiritual warfare and you will get scraped, bruised and battered.

6. I like how Paul put it in 2 Corinthians 4:8-9. Write what you find.

_____

_____

_____

Above All, Taking the Shield of Faith

7. The next piece of armour is described as a top priority. "Above all, taking the shield of faith, wherewith ye shall be able to quench all the fiery darts of the wicked." The shield of faith is given unusually prominent status in the armour of God. Why do you think that is so?

_____

_____

_____

8. We all have choice. We can chose to believe or not believe God. A very precious promise is found in Colossians 2:13-14, which must be claimed by faith and faith alone. Write what you see.

_____

_____

_____

9. Satan presses this type of accusation at us whenever we have fallen; especially when we commit a sin we said we would never do. Ultimately, the objective of the enemy is to get you to quit. Look at two passages: Matthew 26:31-33 and Luke 22:31-34. What happened? Note especially what Christ prayed for Peter.

_____

_____

_____

You see, our High Priest, Jesus Christ, was already praying for Peter and for you and me as well that our faith fail not. He told him that when he was converted or turned again to God in repentance, then he was to go and strengthen his brothers.

10. Look 1 Peter 1:5-7 and see if you can discover what Peter learned.

_____

_____

_____

The next thing to notice about the shield of faith is it quenches all the fiery darts of the wicked. It is interesting to note the word darts. Do any of you know much about darts? How much range do they have? It is very limited, which means these attacks come from close quarters. Also, natives from South America and other parts of Polynesia use blow darts in hunting animals. The darts are dipped in a super toxic nerve poison that kills their prey within seconds. Again, the blow dart has a very limited range and is rather crude by today's standards, but it is absolutely lethal.

The Roman soldiers had very different shields than that of their foes. When they rested them on the ground, the top of their shield was nearly shoulder high. When the soldiers marched and came under attack from the most modern weapon of their day (the spear and arrow), they would put their shields edge-to-edge, forming a protective wall against whatever angle the projectile was coming in on—from flat to near vertical. This reminds us of the protective nature of the body. If one person is weak in faith, then we who are stronger must come along side and raise our shield.

11. Our faith allows us to turn to God for healing. Remember the Israelites who were dying from poisonous, fiery serpents. Notice how God chose to heal them as found in Numbers 21:5-9. What method did He use? Would that be your first choice?

_____

_____

_____

The Helmet of Salvation

The next piece of the armour of God is the helmet of salvation (which could actually be interpreted the hope of salvation (I Thessalonians 5:8)). The helmet is a vital piece of equipment, even today. How many of you had helmets as a little kid when you rode your bike? Most of us never did, yet today, protective helmets save lives. They prevent serious brain injury and incapacitation. Just recently, a famous actress died while learning to ski on the easiest beginners slope. She was not wearing a helmet when she fell. Less than two days later she died due to bleeding in her brain. That is why the helmet of salvation is also critical as we stand against all the assaults of the enemy.

Salvation is one of those terms you need to understand. It means to surround the head with the defense of a Saviour, protection, preservation, or deliverance from the just wrath of God. It has three tenses—I was saved, I am saved, and I will be saved. I was saved from the slavery of sin and was set free so I could chose to serve God. I am saved by the indwelling Spirit who breaks the power of sin over my life, so I can fully serve God. I will be saved is the final phase when we will be resurrected and put on a new body that is incorruptible and are forever with the Lord. Then the very presence of sin is forever banished from our presence.

The Sword of the Spirit—the Word of God

The next piece of armour is the sword of the Spirit, which is the word of God. Most of the armour up to this point has been defensive in nature. However, the sword can be either defensive or offensive. It can be used to wound or slay the enemy or make the enemy stop his attack. It can also block or deflect blows from other weapons the enemy uses. It will cut through nets and trip wires the enemy uses to try and capture us.

12. Look at Hebrews 4:12-16 and put down what you see.

_____

_____

_____

13. As a discerner of the thoughts and intents of the heart, the word of God is the primary tool God uses in healing or removing those infected tumors in our lives. Another description is expressed in John 15:1-5, 8. What technique does God use and why does He do it?

_____

_____

_____

God prunes us so we will be more productive. He is not willing for us just to bear fruit, nor is He willing to stop us at bearing just more fruit. Until we bear <u>much</u> fruit, God is not satisfied with our lives.

Some think we have to use the sword of the Spirit to hack down our brothers and sisters in Christ. We are quick to point out, "Thus saith the Lord." Rather, for those caught in a sin, we who are spiritual have a duty to restore that person in a spirit of meekness, because people who live in glass houses should not throw stones. Rather than tear down, learn to use the word of God to edify—to build up the believers.

14. Look at Galatians 6:1 and Ephesians 4:29-30 and see what principles you uncover.

_____

_____

_____

Praying in the Spirit

15. Many think the armour concludes with the sword of the Spirit. However, there is still one more vital piece to our armour. It is our communication with the Father as we learn to pray in the Spirit. What do you think that means? You may want to look at Romans 8:26-27.

_____

_____

_____

16. Another aspect of our praying in the Spirit is watching with all perseverance and supplication for all saints. While in the garden of Gethsemane, remember Jesus asked the disciples to pray while He was praying a short distance from them. Look at the passage in Matthew 26:37-41 and write what you find.

_____

_____

_____

Again, even our prayer life must rely upon the Spirit. We try hard to pray in our flesh and we fall asleep. We can barely pray for our own needs, yet who we are instructed to watch in prayer over? All of the saints! Lord, help us to pray in your Spirit with watchfulness, perseverance, and supplications for all the saints.

I hope this study has helped you learn what God has already done and blessed us with in Christ— **sit**; and that you have learned how to obey and follow His leading—**walk**, and have come to the point that you will now be able to stand against all the wiles of the devil and having done all— **stand** in the power of His might. Remember, God may call us back to sit and learn and help us adjust our walk in order that we may become a stronger warrior standing against the enemy who wants to kill, steal and destroy. Do all to the glory of God and our Lord and Saviour Jesus Christ. Amen and amen.

About the Author

A 1969 Air Force Academy graduate and B-52 pilot during his career, he began teaching in prisons in 1990. Upon his retirement in 1993, he began asking God, "What's next for my life?" Eight years later in 2001, God answered with one word, "Aftercare", the process of preparing men and women in prison for a successful release back to the community. He currently has a program called "Pathway to Freedom", which is being piloted in three Alabama prisons and is based on biblical principles for spiritual wellness.